Ron Woollacott's
NUNHEAD NOTABLES

John Allan's monument undergoing restoration work in January 2001
See pages 16 and 17

Ron Woollacott's
NUNHEAD NOTABLES

A Biographical List of Notable Men and Women
Buried in London's Nunhead Cemetery of All Saints

Illustrated by the author

Friends of Nunhead Cemetery - London
2002

Copyright (c) Ronald James Woollacott 1984 & 2002

First published 1984
Reprinted (with plan) 1987
Revised and enlarged edition published May 2002

All drawings and photographs are by the author

Published by
The Friends of Nunhead Cemetery
c/o 185 Gordon Road
LONDON,
SE15 3RT

ISBN 0-9539194-3-9

All rights reserved.
No part of this publication may be reproduced
in any form or by any means without the written
permission of the author and publisher.

Printed and bound in Great Britain by Catford Print Centre, London, SE6

INTRODUCTION

When the Friends of Nunhead Cemetery published my original selection of *Nunhead Notables* exactly eighteen years ago, few people realised just how many noteworthy people had been laid to rest in London's Nunhead Cemetery of All Saints. Hitherto, much had been written about the 'famous' buried in the other great 19th century commercial London cemeteries, but for some reason the permanent 'residents' of Nunhead were always overlooked.

The historical writers Thornbury and Walford provided long lists of the eminent persons buried in the cemeteries at Kensal Green, Norwood, Highgate, Brompton and Abney Park, but ignored Nunhead's illustrious dead when compiling *Old and New London*. Edward Walford completed *Old and New London* after Walter Thornbury's death, including the volume containing a few words on Nunhead, but failed to mention a single person buried in the cemetery, despite the fact that Thornbury, his eminent co-writer, had been laid to rest there in 1876.

In recent times too, writers have tended to overlook Nunhead Cemetery. One will search in vain for an entry on Nunhead's dead celebs in *Harrap's Guide to Famous London Graves*; *Permanent Londoners*; and *Who Lies Where - A Guide to Famous Graves,* and Douglas Greenwood mentions just one individual, i.e. Sir Frederick Abel, in his grave guidebook *Who's Buried Where in England*. Hugh Meller lists thirteen people in his 1981 edition of *London Cemeteries*, happily, a recent edition of his excellent cemetery gazetteer includes most of the 140 people featured in the first edition of *Nunhead Notables*.

Nunhead Notables was reprinted in 1987, but has long since been out of print. The preparation of this enlarged and completely revised edition, has provided me with an opportunity to include a number of biographical sketches that were omitted from my first and second selections through lack of space. I have also rewritten and updated each of the existing entries, amending the text where necessary and providing additional information including grave and square numbers.

This new edition of *Nunhead Notables*, together with *More Nunhead Notables* published by the Friends of Nunhead Cemetery in 1995, gives a fascinating insight into the lives of 400 interesting personalities that were laid to rest in Nunhead Cemetery between the years 1840 and 1998. At least fifty of them have entries in the *Dictionary of National Biography,* and many more are featured in Frederic Boase's *Modern English Biography*.

Ron Woollacott

Nunhead, London
December 2001

ACKNOWLEDGMENTS

I first set about exploring the great wooded cemetery at Nunhead in the 1950s. I was fascinated by what I saw and began delving into its history and gathering information about the lives of the many thousands of persons buried there.

I must thank all the kind people who have provided me with information over the years. Everyone has been most friendly and obliging, with the exception, that is, of one casual employee of United Cemeteries (the last private owners of the cemetery) who stopped me copying monumental inscriptions, and accused me of spying for Southwark Council. This sad person believed that copying MIs was disrespectful and tantamount to sacrilege!

Firstly, I should like to thank Mr Terry Connor, Superintendent & Registrar of Southwark Cemeteries, and his predecessors Messrs Arthur Vercouttre, Lou Hedger and Jeff Webber, and all the cemetery staff for their assistance over the years, especially Messrs Chris Barr, Tony Black, Michael Buckley, Bert Evans, Michael O'Shaughnessy and Fred Wilson.

I am especially indebted to the following persons and organisations for answering my numerous enquiries over many years: the Revd J. J. Brown, Secretary, Spurgeon's College; Mrs Jean Chapman, Executive Secretary, Royal Historical Society; Mrs C. T. Clarkson, Archivist, Geological Society of London; Mr John Creasey, Librarian, Dr William's Library; Miss S. Darrell-Brown, Administration Officer, Linnean Society of London; Mr Kenneth Dix, Hon. Secretary, Strict Baptist Historical Society; Mr R. Fish, Librarian, Zoological Society of London; Mr P. D. Hingley, Librarian, Royal Astronomical Society; Mrs Christine Kelly, Archivist, Royal Geographical Society; Mr B. G. Leonard, Secretary, Royal Entomological Society; Miss Linda Martin, SEGAS, Rye Lane, Peckham; Mr W. A. Morris, Archivist, Institution of Civil Engineers; Mr S. G. Morrison, Librarian, Institution of Mechanical Engineers; Mr F. H. Thompson, General Secretary, Society of Antiquaries of London; Mr I. D. Thompson, Guardian Royal Exchange Assurance Group; the Revd J. J. Wortley, Baptist Historical Society; and the Librarian of the Royal Society.

My thanks are also due to the staff of Nunhead Library; the Society of Genealogists; Southwark Local Studies Library; and Westminster Libraries.

Thanks also to Ms Caroline Adams; Dr R. J. Adams; Mrs Elaine Baly aka Vivienne Browning; the late Mr Eric P. Blackwell; Miss Mary Ann Bonney; Mrs Rosemary Burgess; Mr Richard Busby; Mr R. A. Crouch; Mr Harold Finch; Mr Peter Gurnett; Mr Richard Hartree; Mr Roy Hemington; Mr Gordon Johnston; Mr Brian Lancaster; Miss E. McDougall; Mr John Peet; Mrs Laura Probert; the late Mr Eric E. F. Smith FSA; Mr Andrew Waller; and Mr Philip Whittemore.

I am indebted to my wife Maureen, my family and friends and the Friends of Nunhead Cemetery, in particular Mr Jeff Hart and Mr Chris Knowles, for their support and encouragement. Finally, I must thank my daughter Mrs Michele Louise Burford for reading the revised manuscript and for offering useful advice.

ABBREVIATIONS - *General*

aka = also known as
AKCL = Associate of King's College (London)
AMICE = Associate Member of Institution of Civil Engineers
ARSA = Associate of the Royal Scottish Academy
BA = Bachelor of Arts
BD = Bachelor of Divinity
CB = Companion of the Bath
CBE = Commander of the Order of the British Empire
CIE = Companion of the Order of the Indian Empire
CM = Master in Surgery
DCL = Doctor in Civil Law
DD = Doctor in Divinity
D.Litt = Doctor of Letters
D.Sc = Doctor of Science
DSO = Companion of the Distinguished Service Order
FES = Fellow of the Entomological Society
FHS = Fellow of the Horticultural Society
FIA = Fellow of Institute of Actuaries
FCIS = Fellow of the Chartered Institute of Secretaries
FGS = Fellow of the Geological Society
FLS = Fellow of the Linnean Society
FMS = Fellow of the Marine Society
FRAS = Fellow of the Royal Astronomical Society
FRBS = Fellow of the Royal Botanic Society
FRCP = Fellow of the Royal College of Physicians
FRGS = Fellow of the Royal Geographical Society
FRHisS = Fellow of the Royal Historical Society
FRIBA = Fellow of the Royal Institute of British Architects
FRS = Fellow of the Royal Society
FRSanI = Fellow of the Royal Sanitary Institute
FRSL = Fellow of the Royal Society of Literature
FSA = Fellow of the Society of Antiquaries
FSI = Fellow of the Royal Institution of Chartered Surveyors
FSS = Fellow of the Royal Statistical Society
FTCL = Fellow of Trinity College of Music, London
FZS = Fellow of the Zoological Society
GCB = Knight Grand Cross of the Bath
GCVO = Knight Grand Cross of the Royal Victorian Order
GLC = Greater London Council
GPO = General Post Office
ISO = Imperial Service Order
JP = Justice of the Peace
KCB = Knight Commander of the Bath
KTS = Knight of the Tower and Sword
LCC = London County Council
Litt.D = Doctor of Literature
LL.B = Bachelor of Laws
LL.D = Doctor of Laws
LSA = Licentiate of the Society of Apothecaries
MA = Master of Arts
MB = Bachelor of Medicine
MD = Doctor of Medicine
MICE = Member of the Institution of Civil Engineers
MIME = Member of the Institution of Mechanical Engineers
MP = Member of Parliament
MRAS = Member of the Royal Astronomical Society
MRCP = Member of the Royal College of Physicians
Mus.D = Doctor in Music
OBE = Officer of Order of British Empire
PC = Privy Councillor
QC = Queen's Counsel
RCA = Member of the Royal Cambrian Academy
RN = Royal Navy
RNR = Royal Naval Reserve
VD = Volunteer Officer's Decoration

ABBREVIATIONS - *Sources*

Alumni Canta = J. A. Venn, *Alumni Cantabrigienses,* 6 vols, 1922.
Alumni Oxon = J. Foster, *Alumni Oxonienses*, 8 vols, 1887-1892.
BC = *British Census,* various years.
Crockford = *Crockford's Clerical Directory*, various years.
DNB = *Dictionary of National Biography* published in various editions by the Oxford University Press.
KHB = *Kelly's Handbook to the Titled, Landed and Official Classes* 1880 to 1960.
LCC = Manuscript Records of the London Cemetery Company and London Cemetery Company Limited, including *Day Books; Index to Burials at Nunhead Cemetery; Register of Owners of Vaults and Graves; and Directors and Shareholders Minute Books.*
MEB = Frederic Boase, *Modern English Biography,* 6 vols, 1892-1921, and 1965 facsimile edition.
MI = Monumental Inscriptions in Nunhead Cemetery. Private collection of over 4,000 monumental inscriptions transcribed by the author between 1968 and 1990.
WW = *Who's Who,* various years to date.
WWW = *Who Was Who 1897-1995*, 9 volumes.

NUNHEAD CEMETERY - *Historical Background*

The story of Nunhead Cemetery begins with the movement to establish secure, safe and sanitary burial grounds out of town. The first commercial 'London' cemetery was opened at Kensal Green by the General Cemetery Company in November 1832. The success of the cemetery at Kensal Green encouraged the formation of other companies, including the South Metropolitan Cemetery Company and the London Cemetery Company, both of which were incorporated by separate Acts of Parliament in 1836.

The South Metropolitan Cemetery Company opened a cemetery at West Norwood in December 1837, and this was followed by the London Cemetery Company's Highgate Cemetery in May 1839.

Also in 1839 the London Cemetery Company purchased over 130 acres of arable, pasture and meadowland at Nunhead Hill, Camberwell, on the south side of the Thames. About 53 acres were marked out for a cemetery and the rest was sold to a developer. The cemetery was enclosed and laid out with winding gravel paths and thickly planted with trees and shrubs. Two entrance lodges were built in the neo-classical style, and temporary chapels were erected for Anglicans and Dissenters. The cemetery was designed by James Bunstone Bunning who had worked with Stephen Geary at Highgate.

The Nunhead Cemetery of All Saints was consecrated by the Bishop of Winchester in July 1840, with the exception of several acres on the western side which were set aside for the burial of Dissenters and other non-Anglicans.

The first grave space in the consecrated ground was sold to George Long Shand, sailmaker of Bermondsey, and the second was sold to John Tighe of Deptford. The first burial in the unconsecrated section was that of Margaret Austin of Peckham in November 1840. Business was slow during the first year, but by 1843 over 460 burials had taken place. In 1845 two permanent mortuary chapels were built to the designs of Thomas Little.

By 1851, the year of the Great Exhibition in Hyde Park, Nunhead had become a fashionable burial park patronised by the gentry and wealthier classes, including businessmen and tradesmen. Just 20 years later, however, the largely rural district of Nunhead had been overrun by developers and all the fields and meadows had been built upon. These developments, combined with the increased competition from the cheaper parochial cemeteries at Honor Oak and Brockley, had an adverse effect on Nunhead's business. As a result prices were revised; a cheaper class of private grave was introduced, and the charges for common burials were reduced to meet the requirements of the new working class neighbourhood which had sprung near the cemetery.

The early years of the 20th century were the London Cemetery Company's most prosperous, and for a brief period Nunhead was again fashionable. One of the most impressive sights ever seen at Nunhead took place in the autumn of 1908 when Sir George Thomas Livesey, Chairman of the South Metropolitan

Gas Company, was laid to rest in his private burial vault. Over 7,000 people, mainly working men, women and children, lined the route from the Old Kent Road to the cemetery gates. Sir George's monument, a simple red granite obelisk, is located on the east side of the cemetery's main tree-lined avenue.

A large number of bombs fell in the cemetery during World War II causing untold damage to buildings and monuments. The Harris mausoleum on the main avenue was completely demolished along with a linden tree and several more funerary monuments. Part of the boundary wall fronting Linden Grove was also demolished, and the Dissenters' chapel sustained irreparable damage.

After the war the London Cemetery Company was in severe financial trouble and stocks and shares were sold to pay wages and dividends. In 1960, Nunhead and its sister cemetery at Highgate, together with cemeteries in Edinburgh, became part of United Cemeteries, and the old London Cemetery Company ceased to exist.

In 1968 United Cemeteries decided it could no longer keep Nunhead operating as a going concern, and ceased business in February 1969. Within a few years the once impressive cemetery, abandoned and uncared for, became a wilderness. Graves were lost in the undergrowth, thieves helped themselves to valuable artifacts, and vandals went on the rampage. The Anglican chapel, both lodges and the catacombs were broken into, records destroyed, graves desecrated, and human remains disturbed. It was a national disgrace.

In 1974 Southwark councillors met with MPs and ministers and agreed that the problem of Nunhead had to be resolved. In 1975 the Royal Assent was given to a Bill which enabled Southwark Council to take possession. Despite the Council's good intentions the general condition of the cemetery left a lot to be desired. As a result in November 1981 the Friends of Nunhead Cemetery was established, and immediately entered into negotiations with the Council in an attempt to influence the development of the cemetery as a local amenity. In the summer of 1986, over 1,000 visitors attended Nunhead's first 'Open Day' in the cemetery, which was organised jointly by FONC and Southwark Council.

In 1999 Nunhead Cemetery was awarded £1.25 million as a result of a successful FONC/ Southwark Council bid to the Heritage Lottery Fund. Work carried out and completed in 2001 included the restoration of the boundary railings, the chapel and fifty monuments. The cemetery, which is managed jointly by Southwark's Park Rangers and FONC, is much improved as a result.

Nunhead Cemetery is now a Grade II* (starred) historic landscape and the final resting place of over 229,000 persons, including many of local, national and international importance. This book is dedicated to their memory.

NUNHEAD NOTABLES - *The Biographies*

Sir FREDERICK AUGUSTUS ABEL *1st baronet, KCB, GCVO, DCL, D.Sc, FRS* (1827-1902) *Chemist and Explosives Expert*

Frederick Augustus Abel was born in London on the 17 July 1827, the son of Johann Leopold Abel, a German music teacher. He became interested in science as a lad, and entered the Royal College of Chemistry in 1845. He was Professor of Chemistry at the Royal Military Academy, Woolwich from 1852 to 1855, and Chemist to the War Department from 1856 to 1888.

Abel invented cordite and a method of finding the flashpoint of petroleum in association with Professor James Dewar. He published numerous scientific works including: *The Modern History of Gunpowder* (1866); *Gun Cotton* (1866); *On Explosive Agents* (1875); and *Electricity Applied to Explosive Purposes* (1884).

He was President of the Government Committee on Explosives and the first Director of the Imperial Institute. He was elected FRS in 1860. Appointed CB in 1877 and KCB in 1883, he was created a baronet in 1893.

Sir Frederick was twice married. His first wife, Sarah Selina Blanch, whom he married in 1854, died in 1888. He married secondly, in 1889, Giullietta de la Feuillade (see Lady Abel). He died at Westminster, 6 September 1902 and was laid to rest in the crypt of the Anglican chapel..

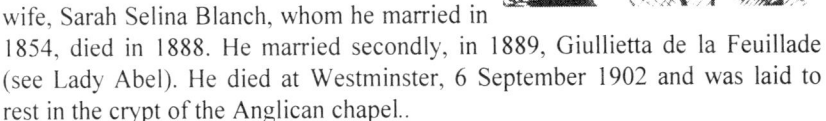

Grave No 26520, Chapel catacomb compartment. Sources: LCC; DNB; KHB; WWW Vol I; BC 1881; *Burke's General Armory* 1884; *Alibone's Dictionary of Authors Supplement* 1891; Fox-Davies A. C. *Armorial Families* 1893; Plarr, Victor G. *Men and Women of Our Time* 1899; *Walford's County Families of the UK* 1901; *Daily Express Encyclopaedia* Vol I 1934.

Lady ABEL (1854-1892) *Baronet's Wife*

Giullietta, Lady Abel, was the daughter of John de la Feuillade, and the second wife of Sir Frederick Augustus Abel (q.v.) whom she married in 1889. She died at 40 Cadogan Place, London in 1892, aged 38 years.

Grave No 20924, Chapel catacomb compartment. Sources: LCC; Fox-Davies A. C. *Armorial Families* 1893; *Walford's County Families of the UK* 1901.

ROBERT ABEL (1857-1936)
aka BOBBY 'THE GUV'NOR' ABEL
Professional Cricketer

Robert Abel was born at 18 Commercial Street, Rotherhithe, on the 30 November 1857, the son of Thomas Abel, a street lamplighter. He practised playing cricket in the grimy streets near the Surrey Commercial Docks before developing his skills on a brand new cricket ground in Southwark Park.

Abel was a hop porter and played cricket for the Borough Hop Trade Cricket Club before joining Surrey County Cricket Club in 1881. The diminutive cricketer first played for England in 1887, and three years later he was named as *Wisden's Cricketer of the Year*. A master batsman, in 1899 he made 357 not out against Somerset at the Oval.

Bobby Abel played for England in thirteen test matches; his first was against Australia at Lords in 1887/8, and his last against Australia at Manchester in 1902. He made 132 not out against Australia at Sydney in 1892. Failing eyesight forced 'The Guv'nor' to retire from first-class cricket in 1904.

He was Surrey coach in 1907, and later ran a cricket shop with his sons near the Oval. He manufactured a bat called *The Guv'nor* and invented a patent cricket ball 'of the softer variety' especially for schoolboys. He was the author of *Cricket and How to Play It* (1894), and *Life and Reminiscences of Robert Abel in the Cricket Field* (1910). He died at his home, 44 Handforth Road, Stockwell, on 10 December 1936, aged 79 years.

Grave 22802 Sq 136, Headstone and curbs. Mason: D. C. Preston & Co, Nunhead. **Sources:** LCC; MI; BC 1881; Grace W. G. *'W.G.' Cricketing Reminiscences and Personal Recollections* 1899; Kent, William *London Worthies* 1939; *Wisden's Cricketer's Almanack* 1980; Kynaston, David *Bobby Abel - Professional Batsman* 1982; Frindall, Bill *Guinness Book of Cricket Facts & Feats* 1983; Green, Benny (ed) *The Wisden Book of Cricketer's Lives* 1986; Frindall, Bill *England Test Cricketers* 1989; Bailey P. Thorn P. and Wynne-Thomas P. *Who's Who of Cricketers* 1993; Paine, Philip *Innings Complete* 1999; Sawyer, David *A Century of Surrey Stumpers* 2001.

~ 14 ~

HENRY ADAMS (1799-1887)
Principal Clerk, Lloyd's Register of Shipping

Henry Adams was born in Lambeth. He commenced work as a clerk in the Underwriters Registry at the age of 14, and was Principal Clerk at Lloyd's Register of British and Foreign Shipping at the time of his death, having served Lloyd's of London for seventy-four years. He died at his residence, 156 Lambeth Road, Lambeth, on 2 April 1887, aged 88 years.
Grave No 2873 Sq 84. *Headstone (with bas-relief of sailing ship).*
Sources: LCC; MI; BC 1881; MEB Vol IV 1908; Wright, C. and Fayle, C.E. *A History of Lloyds* 1928.

Professor HENRY ADAMS *MICE, MIMechE, FSI, FRIBA, FRSanI* (1846-1935)
Consulting Engineer

Henry Adams was born in Limehouse on the 24 March 1846, the eldest son of John Henry Adams, civil engineer. He started work at 15 and gained practical experience in the engineering workshops administered by his father and uncle, before attending King's College and the City of London College. Henry Adams invented the Adams Vortex Blast Pipe for Locomotives whilst working under his uncle, William Adams, who was Locomotive Superintendent of the North London Railway. From 1865 to 1877 he was Outdoor Manager for Sir W. G. Armstrong and Co.

He was for over thirty-five years Professor of Engineering at the City of London College, during which time he gave over 10,000 lectures. He was President of the Civil & Mechanical Engineers Society 1889; President of the Society of Engineers 1890; President of the Institution of Sanitary Engineers 1908; President of the Institution of Engineers-in-Charge 1910; and President of the Institution of Structural Engineers from 1914 to 1916, He was Honorary Member and Gold Medallist of the Institution of Structural Engineers in 1923.

Professor Adams lived for many years at Brockley Park, Forest Hill. Elected a Councillor for the Metropolitan Borough of Lewisham in 1906, he was appointed Chairman of the Works and Highways Committee. He served three years on the Council but declined to be be re-elected because he did not approve of the party tactics employed.

The author of numerous technical publications, Professor Adam's most significant work was probably 'Cassell's Building Construction'. He had a lifelong interest in genealogy, and his autobiography *Some Reminiscences - 75 Years Work in Civil Engineering,* was published in 1925. He died at his residence, The Cedars, 49 Brockley View, London, SE23, on 13 August 1935, aged 89 years.
Grave No 24571 Sq 114. *Marble headstone and curbs (removed 1980 by*

Southwark Council as part of a public park scheme. **Sources:** LCC; BC 1881; WW 1934; WWW Vol III; Letter from Dr R. J. Adams dated 16 May 2000.

JAMES ADAMS (1835-1911)
Engineer and Inventor

James Adams was born at Hayling Island, Hampshire, in January 1835, the son of William Adams, a grocer and brick-maker. The family later removed to Fareham where his father owned a brick kiln. When James was nineteen he removed to London and spent much of his time experimenting with various mechanical inventions. In 1863 he invented and manufactured an 'improved steam boiling indicating apparatus' which he adapted for hotels, hospitals and ships.

In the 1860s he met Isabella Smith from Kidderminster. They married and set up home at Smethwick where in 1869 James secured a job as an engine turner in a local engineering works. In 1882 he left Smethwick with his family and settled in Southwark. One day, while confined to bed with a severe attack of sciatica, a creaky bedroom door gave him an idea which resulted in the invention of a unique door closing spring. Two years later he began manufacturing his patent door spring in a shop in Blackfriars Road.

James Adams was the inventor and 'sole manufacturer' of the 'Slave' single and double action pneumatic door spring and the 'AJ' safety window sash fastener. His patent springs were supplied to numerous institutions, hospitals, hotels and banks, at home and abroad. His practical inventions won several awards including a medal which was presented to him by the Society of Architects at the Building Trades Exhibition 1886.

In about 1903 Adams moved to Ipswich where he opened a small engineering business with his son. He died at 257 Cauldwell Hall Road, Ipswich, Suffolk, 9 June 1911, aged 76 years.

Grave 22645 Sq 119. Headstone and curbstones. NB. In 1984 a stained glass window was erected in the Church of Christchurch, Blackfriars Road, Southwark, to mark the centenary of his firm. **Sources:** LCC; MI; BC 1881; Harris, S. *Old Surviving Firms of South London* 1987; *Trades directories.*

JOHN ALLAN (1790-1865)
Ship Owner

John Allan was born at Whitby, Yorkshire, on the 8 August 1790. Very little is known of his early life other than he was apprenticed to a draper in Whitby and ran away to sea. In later life he was a partner in a shipping firm in the City of London which became John Allan and Sons, and was located at 110 Leadenhall Street. He died at his residence, St John's Villas, Lewisham Road, Deptford, 29 May 1865.

Allan's eldest son and partner, Colonel John Harrison Allan, who was an amateur archaeologist *(*see *More Nunhead Notables)*, rebuilt Ugglebarnby Church, Yorkshire, in memory of his father, and probably designed the massive family tomb at Nunhead, based on the Payava tomb at Xanthos, and erected in 1867. Matthew Noble signs the bronze bas-relief portrait of John Allan at the rear of the monument. John Allan's tomb is without doubt the most expensive monument to be erected at Nunhead.

NB: Another memorial to John Allan - an angel and cross - also by Noble, may be seen in St John's Church, Lewisham Way.

Grave 8617 Sq 68. Large granite monument over vault. Listed Grade II in *1998.* **Sources:** LCC; MI; Dews, Nathan *The History of Deptford in the Counties of Kent and Surrey* 1884; Woollacott, Ron *Interesting Persons Buried at Nunhead No 4 - John Allan,* 'Friends of Nunhead Cemetery Newsletter 5, Summer 1983; Pevsner, N. and Cherry B. *The Buildings of England London 2 South* 1983; Letter from Andrew H. Waller of Andover 1992; *Trades directories.*

Dr ROBERT ARCHIBALD ARMSTRONG *MA, LL.D* (1788-1867)
Gaelic Lexicographer to King George IV

Robert Archibald Armstrong was born at Kenmore, Perthshire in 1878, the eldest son of Robert Armstrong. He was educated by his father and later at Edinburgh and at St Andrew's University. In 1825 he published *A Gaelic Dictionary,* which was the first ever Gaelic dictionary published. In 1826 he was appointed Gaelic Lexicographer in Ordinary to George IV.

Dr Armstrong kept several high class schools in the vicinity of London. He founded the South Lambeth Grammar School in 1830, of which establishment he was headmaster until his retirement in 1852. He was the author of several articles on meteorological matters published in *Arcana of Science and Art* from 1837 onwards. He died at his residence, Hanover House, Choumert Road, Peckham, on 25 May 1867.

Grave 9535 Sq 70. Pedestal (in ruins). **Sources:** LCC; MI; DNB; MEB Vol I 1892.

Mrs MARGARET AUSTIN (1804-1840)
First Person to be interred in the Dissenters' Ground

Margaret Austin was the wife of the Reverend John Baptist Austin, a Nonconformist Minister of Goldsmith House, Peckham. She died on the 14 November 1840, aged 36 years. Mrs Austin was the first person to be buried in the unconsecrated or Dissenters' ground at Nunhead.

Grave No 5 Sq 161. Headstone (laid down). **Sources:** LCC; MI.

Revd CHARLES WATERS BANKS (1806-1886)
Strict Baptist Preacher, Printer and Publisher

Charles Waters Banks was born at Ashford, Kent, on the 9 February 1806. At the age of seven he was sent to live with his maternal grandfather, Samuel Waters, at Cranbrook, Kent. His grandfather was a printer and young Master Banks learnt the art of printing on his grandfather's wooden press, printing and publishing the first provincial magazine, *The Weald of Kent Mirror,* when he was just 17 years of age.

In 1827 he removed to Canterbury and printed *The Penny Sunday Reader*, the first Church of England penny paper. He also printed and published *The Kentish Times*, *The Kentish Observer* and another two newspapers.

Charles Waters Banks became a Strict Baptist Minister and removed to London. In 1841 he preached the Gospel for the first time in a house in Bermondsey. In 1845 he founded *The Earthen Vessel*, a magazine for Strict Baptists, which was distributed throughout the English speaking world. He was a Minister of Religion for sixty years and preached in virtually every county in England and Wales. His book, *The Life and Times of John Calvin*, was published in 1851.

The diminutive Mr Banks - he was only 5ft 3ins tall - was a big-hearted man. He gave generously to those in need, particularly to widows and orphans, and died virtually penniless at 9 Banbury Road, Hackney, on 25 March 1886. He was laid to rest on 2 April 1886. Hundreds of mourners attended his funeral, and 36 Baptist ministers took part in the service at his grave.

Grave No 2516 Sq 115. Marble pedestal and urn *(damaged - urn missing). Mason: D. C. Preston, Nunhead. Erected by public subscription.* **Sources:** LCC; MI; BC 1881; MEB Vol IV 1908; *The Earthen Vessel* (Obituary) May 1886; Dix, Kenneth *Particular Baptists and Strict Baptists - An Historical Survey* Strict Baptist Historical Society's Annual Report 1976.

EDWARD HARTNELL BARTLETT (1837-1923)
Former Secretary of Spurgeon's Pastors' College

Edward Hartnell Bartlett was born at Camberwell, the son of Lavinia Strickland Bartlett (q.v.), a Baptist teacher. Originally a Bible Class Leader at the Metropolitan Tabernacle, Newington, he became Secretary of Spurgeon's Tabernacle and Pastors' College, a position he held for forty years. In 1877 he published *Mrs Bartlett and her Class* a tribute to his mother who died in 1875. He died at 52 Tierney Road, Streatham on 10 January 1923, aged 86 years.

Grave 13452 Sq 166. Pedestal *(in ruins).* **Sources:** LCC; MI; BC 1881; Letter from the Revd J. J. Brown, Secretary of Spurgeon's College 21 August 1981.

Mrs LAVINIA STRICKLAND BARTLETT (1806-1875)
Teacher at Spurgeon's Tabernacle

Mrs Bartlett was born at Preston Candover, Hampshire, on the 27 November 1806. She joined the Baptist Church in 1828, and in 1859 she began teaching at New Park Street School, Newington, with a class of just three girls. Mrs Bartlett was a devout, dedicated and popular teacher and her class soon outgrew its accommodation. On removing to the lecture hall at Spurgeon's Metropolitan Tabernacle at the Elephant and Castle, upwards of 700 students regularly attended her class. Despite failing health she continued to teach right up to the time of her death which occurred at 56 New Street, Newington, on 2 August 1875.

NB: The Revd Dr Charles Haddon Spurgeon said Mrs Bartlett was his best deacon and wrote the following inscription over her grave: *'The pastors, deacons and elders of the church in the Metropolitan Tabernacle unite with her class, and the students of the college, in erecting this memorial to her surpassing worth. She was indeed a mother in Israel.'*

Grave 13452 Sq 166. Pedestal and urn *(ruins).* **Sources:** LCC; MI; MEB Vol I 1892; Spurgeon, S. and Harrald, J. (editors) *C. H. Spurgeon Autobiography - The Full Harvest 1860-1892* 1973; Dallimore, Arnold *Spurgeon - A New Biography* 1984.

STANLEY KAY BAWDEN (1866-1933)
Editor of 'The Kentish Mercury' 1915-33

Stanley Kay Bawden was born in Douglas, Isle of Man, in January 1866, the son of Thomas Bawden. He was proud of his Manx connections but his roots were in Cornwall. His grandfather, Edward Bawden, trained at the Cornish School of Mines, and removing to the Isle of Man in 1830, became a miner in the Manx mines retiring in 1864 as Captain of the Foxdale Mines.

Stanley Bawden was educated at King William's College, IOM, and spent some time with the 'Isle of Man Times'. After his marriage to Jessie Kinley of Douglas in 1890, he became the proprietor and editor of the 'Peel City Guardian'. He later sold his business and removed to the mainland.

In 1896 he was appointed chief reporter of 'The Kentish Mercury', and was editor from 1915 to 1933, during which time, the newspaper, under his direction, became one of the most influential London journals outside Fleet Street. He died at 188a Lewisham High Road, Deptford, on Saturday, 2 December 1933, aged 67 years.

NB: His son, Harold Bawden (d.1969), was a reporter on 'The Kentish Mercury' and succeeded his father as editor from 1933 to 1955.

Grave No 38389 Square 77. Headstone. Sources: LCC; 'The Kentish Mercury' 8 December 1933; Information from Mr R. A. Crouch 26 June 2000.

WILLIAM BEARDMORE *AMICE* (1824-1877)
Marine and Civil Engineer

William Beardmore was born at Greenwich on the 6 May 1824, the son of Joseph Beardmore, Engineer to the General Steam Navigation Company. He was apprenticed to his father employed in the construction of marine engines at the Stowage, Deptford, and in 1850, at the age of 26, he was appointed Managing Engineer to the General Steam Navigation Company. He was elected Associate Member of the Institution of Civil Engineers in 1860.

From 1861 to 1877 Beardmore was a partner in the Parkhead Rolling Mill and Forge at Glasgow. He was a brother-in-law to the Revd William George Martin (q.v.). He died at 118 King's Road, Brighton, Sussex, on 11 October 1877, aged 53 years.

NB: The Parkhead Forge was taken over by his son William Beardmore, later Baron Invernairn of Strathnairn (1856-1936), who founded William Beardmore & Co, famous for building battleships, submarines, motor-cars, and the R34, the first airship to make a double crossing of the Atlantic.

Grave 12599 Sq 124. Large funerary monument and scroll over brick vault. *H. Daniel, Nun-Head.* **Sources:** LCC; MI; DNB (William Beardmore junior); MEB Vol I 1892; Letter from the Institution of Civil Engineers.

JOHN BEATSON (1802-1858)
Shipbreaker and Timber Merchant

John Beatson was the son of David Beatson, a Scotsman, who settled in Rotherhithe about 1790. John Beatson inherited his father's shipbreaking business and ran it until his death which occurred at the entrance to the Surrey Commercial Docks, Rotherhithe, on 26 July 1858. Among the many ships broken up in Beatson's yards was the *Temeraire* which had seen service at the Battle of Trafalgar in 1805, and was immortalised by Turner in his famous painting 'The Fighting Temeraire'.

Grave 4790 Sq 109. Obelisk over brick vault. Sources: LCC; MI; Trades directories; Boast, Mary *The Story of Rotherhithe* 1980; Humphrey, Stephen *The Story of Rotherhithe* 1997 pp 27-28.

Revd EDWARD GEORGE AMBROSE BECKWITH *MA* (1795-1856)
Minor Canon of St Paul's and Westminster Abbey

Edward George Ambrose Beckwith was the son of the Revd Edward James Beckwith, a Minor Canon of St Paul's Cathedral and Westminster Abbey. He was educated at St Paul's School, and Lincoln and Magdalene Colleges, Oxford. He was for many years twelfth Minor Canon of St Paul's Cathedral and Sub-chanter from 1850 to death, and a Minor Canon of Westminster Abbey

from 1825 to 1856. He was Rector of St Michael, Bassishaw, in the City of London from 1835 to death. He died in the Little Cloisters, Westminster Abbey on 27 September 1856, aged 61years.
   Grave 3821 Sq 109. Tomb (not found). **Sources:** LCC; MEB Vol IV 1908; *Alumni Oxon; Crockford.*

FREDERICK EDWARD BECKWITH (1821-1898)
World Champion Swimmer known as 'PROFESSOR BECKWITH'

Frederick Edward Beckwith was born at Ramsgate, Kent on the 16 December 1821. At the age of 17 he swam his very first race in the Serpentine at Hyde Park under the auspices of the National Swimming Society. In 1848 he beat Walker, Champion of the North of England.

Beckwith assumed the title of World Champion in August 1851, but was beaten by Young and Steadman in a 400 yards championship race at the Holborn Baths. In 1854 he again assumed the world title.

Beckwith was Superintendent of Lambeth Baths, Westminster Bridge Road, for twenty-five years, from 1850 to 1875. He was also swimming instructor to several colleges and trained many champion swimmers, including Captain Matthew Webb, whom he coached for his successful cross channel swim in 1875. When Captain Webb lost his life at Niagara Falls in 1883, Professor Beckwith, as he was known, organised a special benefit at Lambeth Baths to raise money for the captain's widow and children. On that occasion the professor performed a display of ornamental swimming while wearing full evening dress and a top hat! Willie Beckwith (q.v.) also took part in the event together with his sister Agnes, watched over by a wax effigy of Captain Webb which had been loaned especially for the event by Madame Tussaud's.

After a brief period in retirement as a publican, Professor Beckwith returned to swimming and put on displays with his family at the Royal Aquarium, Westminster. He was appointed swimming instructor to the Uppingham School just two weeks before his death from apoplexy at Leamington Terrace, Uppingham, Leicestershire on 29 May 1898. He was 77 years old.
   Grave 13506 Sq 48. Headstone (sloping forward). Inscription barely legible. **Sources:** LCC; MI; BC 1881; 'The Sporting Life' 7th and 8th June 1898; MEB Vol IV 1908; Watson, Kathy *The Crossing - The curious story of*

[Captain Webb] the first man to swim the English Channel 2000; Information from Roy Hemington.

WILLIAM HENRY BECKWITH (1857-1892)
Champion Swimmer aka WILLIE BECKWITH

A son of Frederick Edward Beckwith (q.v.), William Henry Beckwith was born in Lambeth on the 7 August 1857. He was taught to swim by his father, and at the age of five was taking part in swimming displays with his family at the Lambeth Baths billed as *'Baby Beckwith, the Wonder of the World'*.

Willie Beckwith, as he was better known, won the captaincy of the Serpentine Club in June 1874, and became a champion swimmer. He beat Captain Matthew Webb in a six day race of ten hours a day at the Royal Aquarium, Westminster, in June 1881. He was then lodging at the Feather's Tavern, Wandsworth.

Willie Beckwith received a benefit at the Canterbury Music Hall on the 5 December 1892, and died of bronchitis eight days later at 186 Kennington Road, aged 35 years.

Grave 13506 Sq 48. Headstone *(weathered)*. **Sources:** LCC; MI; BC 1881; MEB Vol IV 1908.

PIO GIOVANNI MICHELL BELLINI (1824-1858)
Composer and Singer

A native of Milan, Pio Giovanni Michell Bellini, was the first husband of the singer and actress Cicely Nott (q.v.) whom he married at Edinburgh in 1856. Signor Bellini, who was a vocalist and musical composer, died at 22 Marlborough Place, Brighton, Sussex on 5 October 1858, aged 34 years.

Grave 2378 Sq 125. Headstone, curbs and iron rails. *Mason: H. Daniel, Nun-Head.* **Sources:** LCC; MI; MEB (under Cicely Nott).

EDWARD THOMAS EDMONDS BESLEY QC (1826-1901)
Recorder of Bury St Edmunds

Edward Thomas Edmonds Besley was born at Exeter, Devon, on the 11 August 1826, the only son of Thomas Besley (q.v.). He was educated at Exeter Free Grammar School, and became a law journalist. He was a Reporter in the Gallery for *The Morning Chronicle* and *The Times* from 1851 to 1864. He was admitted a student of the Middle Temple, and called to the Bar in 1859.

Edward Besley practised at the Central Criminal Court (Old Bailey), and on the Home and South-Eastern Circuits. He was appointed Recorder of Bury St Edmunds in 1892 and took silk in 1894. He was a director of the Lambeth Water Works and several gas companies.

Edward Besley was twice married. His first wife Dorcas, whom he married in 1847, died in 1855. His second wife, Julia, whom he married in 1857, was a daughter of the actor Julio Henry Hughes (see *More Nunhead Notables*). He died at his residence, Rose Mount, 65 Sydenham Hill, 18 September 1901, aged 75 years.

Grave 10521 Sq 27. Small cross *(in ruins)*. **Sources:** LCC; MI; BC 1881; WWW Vol I; KHB 1895.

THOMAS BESLEY (1791-1857)
Newspaper Proprietor and Publisher

Thomas Besley (father of the above) was born on the 27 October 1791. He was the owner and publisher of the *Devonshire Chronicle and Exeter News*. His younger brother, Alderman Robert Besley, was Lord Mayor of London 1869-70. He died at his residence in the Clapham Road, Lambeth, on 19 July 1857, aged 65 years.

Grave 3546 Sq 27. Small cross *(ruins)*. **Sources:** LCC; MI; WWW Vol I.

Revd FREDERICK ATKINS BILLING LL.D, FGS, FRSL, FRHisS, AKC (1829-1910)
Congregational Minister

Frederick Atkins Billing was born at East Haddon, Northamptonshire. He was educated at Guisborough College and King's College, London, and received his LL.D from Maryville, USA. He was a Fellow of several learned societies and an Associate of the Philosophical Society.

In 1872 Dr Billing became interested in the work of the Commercial Dock Congregational Church at Russell Street, Rotherhithe. Having abandoned his original intention of entering the Ministry of the Church of England, in 1874 he accepted the pastorate of Southwark Park Congregational Church. For over thirty years he ministered at Southwark Park without payment of any kind. Poor health compelled him to retire from the ministry in 1906, and he died at his residence, 7 St Donatt's Road, New Cross, on 7 June 1910, aged 81years.

Grave 26797 Sq 145. Monument over brick vault. Sources: LCC; MI; BC 1881; Cleal, Edward E. *The Story of Congregationalism in Surrey* 1908 p 127; *Congregational Year Book* 1911 p 161.

JAMES ALBERT BIRCH (1840-1895)
Gentleman of HM Chapels Royal and Temperance Worker

James Albert Birch was born in 1840 in Sheffield, Yorkshire. He was an accomplished musician, chorister and a Gentleman of HM Chapels Royal, and the founder and conductor of the National Temperance Choral Union and the Temperance Choral Society. He died at 3 Beach Terrace, Hastings, Sussex, on 21 June 1895, aged 55 years.

Grave 22566 Sq 127. Obelisk (collapsed). The base of the monument bears the inscription: 'Erected by his many friends in recognition of his devoted efforts to improve temperance music'. **Sources:** LCC; MI; BC 1881.

Miss ADA BLANCHE (1863-1953)
Singer and Actress

Ada Blanche was the stage name of Ada Blanche Adams. She was born in Brixton in 1863, the eldest daughter of Samuel Adams (1837-1893), a well-known London theatre owner, and his actress wife Sarah Ann Adams, otherwise known as Cicely Nott (q.v.).

Miss Blanche was for many years a principal boy at the Drury Lane Theatre, London. In 1921 she appeared at the Empire Theatre with Thorpe Bates in Montague Phillips's light romantic opera *The Rebel Maid.*

She died in St Joseph's Hospital, Chiswick, 1 January 1953, aged 90 years, and was buried in the family grave at Nunhead.

Grave 25248 Sq 125. Headstone. **Sources:** LCC; MI; BC 1881; *Whitaker's Almanac* 1922; Chance-Newton, H. *Idols of the Halls* 1975.

JOHN BOAK (1837-1876)
Professional Cricketer

John Boak was born in Scotland on the 27 June 1837, and received his education at the Royal High School in Edinburgh. In 1858, at the age of twenty-one, he emigrated to Australia and became a professional cricketer. He played for New South Wales and Queensland, but not in first class matches, before returning to Great Britain in 1868.

A tail-end right-hand batsman and right-arm fast bowler, Boak played just one match for Middlesex County Cricket Club in 1873. He was struck by a train and killed while crossing the railway line at Bermondsey on the 29 October 1876, aged 39 years.

Grave 14101 Sq 13. Common grave (unmarked). **Sources:** LCC; Bailey P. Thorn P. and Wynne-Thomas P. *Who's Who of Cricketers* 1993.

Mrs FRANCES ELIZABETH BRISTOW (1807-1911)
Centenarian

Frances Elizabeth Bristow was born in Greenwich. She was the widow of Henry Essex Bristow of Greenwich, a Berlin wool importer in the City of London. Colonel William Bristow VD (q.v.), and the Revd Richard Rhodes Bristow MA, Canon Missioner of Southwark Cathedral, were her sons. Mrs Bristow died at 117 High Road, Lee, on 30 May 1911, aged 104 years.
   Grave 6527 Sq 93. Box tomb. **Sources:** LCC; MI; BC 1881.

Colonel WILLIAM BRISTOW *VD* (1834-1896)
Solicitor and Officer of Volunteers

William Bristow was born at Greenwich, the 2nd son of Henry Essex Bristow, a Berlin wool merchant, and Frances Elizabeth Bristow (q.v.). As a young man he was articled to his uncle, Alfred Rhodes Bristow, a solicitor and former MP for Kidderminster. He served as Vestry Clerk to the Parish of Greenwich, and Solicitor to the Admiralty and to the Royal Naval Hospital, Greenwich.

As a volunteer officer he was Colonel-in-Chief of the 2nd Volunteer Battalion, Queen's Own Royal West Kent Regiment, and received the Volunteer Officers' Decoration for Long Service. Colonel Bristow resided at 'Woodlands', Mycene Road, Westcombe Park, Blackheath, and died 23 May 1896, aged 62 years. Over 300 members of the local militia mounted guard of honour at his funeral.
   Grave 6527 Sq 93. Box tomb over brick grave. **Sources:** LCC; MI; BC 1881; Rhind, Neil *Blackheath Village & Environs 1790-1970* Vol II 1983 pp 276 and 292; *Trades directories.*

Revd GEORGE MOSS BROCK-ARNOLD *MA, FRHisS* (1847-1888)
Anglican Priest and Historian

George Moss Brock-Arnold was born in Liverpool, the son of Dr Thomas Brock-Arnold, physician. He was educated at King's College, London; Jesus College, Cambridge; and Hertford College, Oxford, and took orders in 1876. He was Curate of St Paul's, Oxford from 1876 to 1878; Curate of Buckland from 1879 to 1880; Curate-in-Charge of Marston Montgomery, Derbyshire in 1881; and Curate of St Anne's, Soho from 1884 to 1885. He was appointed Chaplain of Camberwell Workhouse and Infirmary in 1886.

He was the author of *Oxford Concordance to the Holy Scriptures* and *Gainsborough and Constable.* He died at Brunswick Square, Camberwell, on 3 February 1888, aged 41 years.
   Grave No 19049 Sq 20. Headstone. **Sources:** LCC; MI; BC 1881; *Alumni Canta; Alumni Oxon; Crockford* 1887.

SAMUEL BROOME *FHS* (1805-1870)
Gardener to the Honourable Society of the Inner Temple

Samuel Broome was born on the 29 June 1805, and for much of his life he resided and worked in the City of London. He was a Fellow of the Horticultural Society of London, and for more than 40 years Gardener to the Honourable Society of the Inner Temple. Broome's Annual Chrysanthemum Show brought a wealth of brilliant colour to the grey and grimy streets of Victorian London, and 'gave such valuable testimony to the effects of Lord Palmerston's Smoke Act'.

He died at No 7 Crown Office Row, Temple, on 22 January 1870, aged 64 years. His obituary appeared in the satirical magazine *Punch* on the 5 February 1870, accompanied by the following verse:

> *Farewell to thee, kind, honest, old Sam Broome*
> *In bouton's d'or above thee bloom the mould -*
> *No London Smoke distress thee in the tomb,*
> *and whoso'er i' the Temple fill thy room,*
> *May the new Broom sweep clean as did the old.*

Grave 10774 Sq 83. Obelisk over brick vault. *'Erected by his florist friends'.* **Sources:** LCC; MI; Trade Directories; 'Punch' 5th Feb 1870; Information from Ms Mary Anne Bonney.

HORACE TABBERER BROWN *LL.D, FRS* (1848-1925)
Chemist & Brewer

Horace Tabberer Brown was born at Burton-on-Trent, Staffordshire, on the 20 July 1848. His father, Benjamin Tabberer, died before he was born. He later assumed the surname of his stepfather, Edwin Brown, a naturalist. He was educated at Burton-on-Trent and Atherstone Grammar Schools, and the Royal College of Chemistry. In 1866 he joined Worthington's Brewery as junior brewer and by 1881 he was managing brewer. He was engaged in brewing at Burton-on-Trent until 1893.

A pioneer in the investigations and behaviour of carbohydrates, he was elected FRS in 1889. He received the Longstaff Medal of the Chemical Society in 1894, and served as Vice-President of the Chemical Society from 1894 to 1897. In 1901 he acquired a winery farm in South Africa and introduced many improvements to wine making.

Dr Brown became Governor of the Imperial College of Science and Technology, South Kensington, and published numerous papers on chemical, biological and geological subjects in the *Transactions of the Chemical Society*, *Proceedings of the Royal Society,* etc. He died at 5 Evelyn Gardens, South

Kensington, on 6 February 1925, aged 76 years.
Grave 32177 Sq 77. Headstone. **Sources:** LCC; MI; BC 1881; Proceedings of the Royal Society 'A' 109; Plarr, Victor G. *Men and Women of the Time* 1899; WWW Vol II.

Mrs SARAH ANNA BROWNING (c1773-1849)
Robert Browning's Mother

Sarah Anna Browning was a daughter of William Wiedemann, a Dundee shipowner of German descent. Sarah Anna and her sister Christianna settled in Camberwell in the late 1780s. In 1821 Sarah Anna married Robert Browning, a clerk at the Bank of England, and they had two children: Robert, the poet, was born in 1812 when Sarah was nearly 40 years old, and Sarianna arrived two years later. In 1840 the family removed to Hatcham (New Cross).

Mrs Browning was an accomplished pianist and a devoutly religious woman. She was a member of the York Street Independent Chapel, Walworth from her arrival in Camberwell until her death which occurred suddenly at her residence, Telegraph Cottage, Hatcham on 18 March 1849.

Grave 1307 Sq 79. Headstone (removed to the Browning Collection, Walworth in 1982). **Sources:** LCC; MI, Orr, Mrs Sutherland *Life and Letters of Robert Browning* 1891; Browning, Vivienne *My Browning Family Album* 1979; Thomas, Donald *Robert Browning - A Life Within Life* 1982; Calcraft, Mairi *Robert Browning's London, Browning Society Notes* Vol 19 1989.

WILLIAM SHERGOLD BROWNING (1797-1874)
Historical Writer

William Shergold Browning was a son of Robert Browning of the Bank of England, and a favourite half-uncle to Robert Browning, the poet. William worked with his father in the Bank of England until 1824 when he obtained a position with the Rothschild Bank in Paris.

He was the author of a number of books about historical subjects including, *A History of the Huguenots during the Sixteenth Century,* which was first published in 1829 and went through several editions. His historical novel, *The Provost of Paris,* appeared in 1833, and *Hoel Morvan, or the Court and Camp of Henry V,* was published in 1844. He also wrote *Leisure Hours,* a collection of miscellanies, and was a contributor for some years to the *Gentleman's Magazine.* William Browning returned to England in 1845, and died at Wren Road, Camberwell, on 4 March 1874, aged 77 years.

Grave 4437 Sq 79. Headstone. **Sources:** LCC; MI; MEB Vol I 1892; Orr, Mrs Sutherland *Life & Letters of Robert Browning* 1891; Kirstner, Elvan (ed) *The Letters of RB & EBB 1845-1846* 1969; Browning, Vivienne *My Browning Family Album* 1979.

Lieut-Colonel **ARTHUR CARLYON BRUCE** *OBE, APD* **(1853-1921)**
Army Paymaster

Arthur Carlyon Bruce was born in Scotland on the 27 April 1853. He served in the 60th Rifles and the Army Pay Department from 1878. He was on the staff of the War Office from 1897 to 1919, and worked in the Financial Secretary's Department from 1914 to 1919. Colonel Bruce died at his residence, 246 Ivydale Road, Waverley Park, Nunhead, on 1 May 1921, aged 61 years.
    Grave 34195 Sq 50. Cross on stepped base (demolished). **Sources:** LCC; MI; BC 1881; *Burke's Handbook to the Order of the British Empire* 1921; *Whitaker's Peerage, etc.,* 1921.

Lieut-Colonel **HERBERT BRUCE** *CB* **(1827-1866)**
Former Chief of the Secret Intelligence Department, Indian Army

Herbert Bruce was a son of Major General Sir Charles Bruce KCB who died in 1832 when Herbert was 5 years old. In 1842, at the age of 15, he joined the Bombay Army and was a Captain in the European Regiment in 1855. He saw action during the Indian Mutiny and became Chief of the Secret Intelligence Department. He was appointed CB in 1858.
    Colonel Bruce, who was a serving officer in the Bombay Staff Corps at the time of his death, died on board the SS *Messageries Imperiales* at Suez on the 25 February 1866, aged 39 years. His body was removed from Alexandria and buried at Nunhead in grave number 6705 square 79. In 1872 his remains were exhumed and deposited in a new family vault east of the Anglican chapel.
    Grave 10350 Sq 91. Ledger over vault. **Sources:** LCC; MI; MEB Vol I 1892.

Sir **ERNEST ALFRED THOMPSON WALLIS BUDGE**
MA, Litt.D, D.Litt, FSA **(1857-1934)** *Assyriologist and Egyptologist*

Ernest Budge was born at Bodmin, Cornwall, the son of Quaker parents, on the 27 July 1857. He was educated privately and at Christ's College, Cambridge, where he became Assyrian Scholar and won the Tyrwhitt Hebrew Scholarship in 1882. In 1883 he was appointed assistant in the Oriental Antiquities Department at the British Museum, and was put in charge of the department in 1892. He was appointed Keeper of Egyptian and Assyrian Antiquities in 1894, a position he retained until his retirement in 1924.
    As a collector for the British Museum he made numerous expeditions to the Middle East. He excavated at Assuan and examined sites in the Sudan from 1887 to 1905. It was during an expedition to the Sudan that he contracted glaucoma and lost the sight of an eye. He brought to England many ancient relics including a collection of documents known as the Amarna Tablets.

Sir Wallis Budge, who received his knighthood in 1920, was the author of over 110 works. His first book, *Assyrian Incantations* was published in 1878, and his last, *From Fetish to God in Ancient Egypt,* was published in 1934. He died at his residence, 48 Bloomsbury Street, London, 23 November 1934, aged 77 years.

Grave 34316 Sq 36. Small cross. **Sources:** LCC; MI; BC 1881; DNB; Proceedings of Society of Antiquaries, Vol 15, 1935; *Daily Express Encyclopaedia* Vol 2 1934; WW 1934; WWW Vol 3; Mee, Arthur *Arthur Mee's London* 1937; Ceram, C. W. (ed) *The World of Archaeology* 1966.

Lady BUDGE (1859-1926)

Lady Budge was born Dora Helen Emmerson in Northumberland, the daughter of the Revd Titus Emmerson, Rector of Allendale. At the age of 22 she was an art student and lived with her widowed mother at Pelham Street, Kensington. She married Ernest Alfred Thompson Wallis Budge (q.v.) in 1888. Lady Budge died at 48 Bloomsbury Street, London, 18 October 1926, aged 67 years.

Grave 34316 Sq 36. Small cross. **Sources:** LCC; MI; BC 1881; DNB.

CHARLES BURLS (1814-1896)
Former Secretary to the London Cemetery Company

Charles Burls was born in Walthamstow on the 9 April 1814. He was Clerk to the London Cemetery Company (owners of Nunhead and Highgate cemeteries) in 1842, and was Secretary to the Company from 1843 to 1847. He was Secretary to the Chartered Gas Company in 1848, and Secretary to a Friendly Society at the time of his retirement in 1880.

Burls was a resident of Camberwell for many years, and served his adopted parish as a Guardian of the Poor. He was married to Mary Grant, a daughter of the Revd James Sherman of Blackheath. He died at his residence, the Red House, 218 Peckham Rye, on 7 August 1896, aged 82 years.

Grave 6810 Sq 143. Obelisk over brick grave. **Sources:** LCC; MI; British Census 1881; Blanch, William Harnett *Ye Parish of Camberwell* 1875 pp 185 & 323; *Kelly's PO Directories* 1842 to 1873.

JOSEPH BURTT (1818-1876)
Archaeologist and Assistant Keeper in the National Record Office

Joseph Burtt was born in St Pancras, Middlesex, on the 7 November 1818, and was educated by his father, a tutor and Greek scholar. At the age of 14 he was employed in making inventories of national records housed in the Chapter House, Westminster Abbey. In 1840 he became a clerk in the National Record Office, and in 1851 he was appointed a second-class assistant-keeper of records, and a first class assistant keeper of records in 1859. He organised and superintended the removal of vast quantities of old documents from Westminster Abbey to a new building in Fetter Lane, in the City of London. He was also employed by Dean Stanley in sorting and arranging the muniments of Westminster Abbey. In 1862 he became Secretary of the Royal Archaeological Institute. He was editor of the 'Archaeological Journal', and contributed a number of archaeological and historical papers to the 'Gentleman's Magazine', the 'Athenaeum', and other publications.

He died at his residence, Crofton Lodge, 51 Upper Tulse Hill, Lambeth, on 15 December 1876, aged 58 years, and was buried at Nunhead on the 22 December.

Grave 14186 Sq 31. Head and Foot Stones *(removed by Southwark Council in 1978).* **Sources:** LCC; MEB Vol I. 1892; DNB; Letter from Mr John Peet.

Count CALLIMACHI D.Sc (1861-1931)
Consulting Engineer

Count (Michel) Callimachi was a Consulting Engineer with offices in London and Paris. He resided at No 18 Yeoman's Row, South Kensington, and died in King's College Hospital, Denmark Hill, on 22 October 1931, aged 70 years.

Grave 37737 Sq 39. Headstone. Sources: LCC; MI; *Kelly's PO Directories.*

JOHN CALLOW OWS (1822-1878)
Landscape Artist

John Callow was born at Greenwich on the 19 July 1822, a son of Robert Callow, and the younger brother of the well-known landscape artist William Callow. He was a pupil of his brother who took him to Paris at the age of 13. After studying art in Paris for nine years, he returned to England. In 1855 he was appointed Professor of Drawing at the Royal Military Academy, Addiscombe. He was later appointed Sub-Professor of Drawing at Woolwich.

Callow was a popular art teacher, and taught privately and in many colleges. As an artist he mostly painted marine subjects and landscapes in water colours. He exhibited at the Royal Academy, the British Institute, and the Suffolk Street Gallery from 1844 to 1867. He died of consumption at 35 Lewisham High Road, Lewisham on 25 April 1878, aged 55 years.

NB: Most of his paintings were sold by auction after his death. In 1975 his watercolour *Shipping off Dover* was priced at £365 by Spinks, and his oil painting *A Frigate Entering Port,* was on sale at the Parker Gallery for £750.

Grave 14867 Sq 74. Ledger. Sources: LCC; MI; DNB; MEB Vol I 1892; Bury, Adrian (ed) *Old Water Colour Society's Club 53rd Annual Volume* 1978.

JAMES CAMPBELL (1816-1881)
Engineer whose father was a Claimant to the Earldom of Annandale

James Campbell was born in Edinburgh, a great-grandson of Dougal Campbell of Glensaddle, and Mary, daughter of John Lindsay, Earl of Craufurd. His father Dr Dougal Campbell MD of Newfield, surgeon and physician, was an unsuccessful claimant to the Earldom of Annandale.

James Campbell was a consulting civil engineer and iron shipbuilder whose business premises were at Lothbury in the City of London. He died at his residence 'Annandale' 34 Lee Park, Lee, on 4 October 1881, aged 65 years.

Grave plots 858 and 1861 Sq 96. Ledger. **Sources:** LCC; MI; BC 1881; *Burke's Peerage and Baronetage* 1866; *Trades directories*.

HENRY CAPEL (1795-1887)
Historian of the Worshipful Company of Coopers

Henry Capel was born at Kempsey, Worcestershire, in 1795. He became a wine merchant in the City of London, and was admitted to the Worshipful Company of Coopers in 1827, serving as Warden and Master. In 1831 he became a Member of the Coopers' Society, and was President of the Coopers' Society from 1836 to 1839, and Vice-President from 1845 to 1848. He was also active in local politics and served as a Common Councillor for Tower Ward.

Henry Capel was the author of *Historical Memoranda of the Coopers' Company,* a large manuscript volume comprising some 548 pages.

After residing many years at 'The Limes', Queen's Road, Peckham, he removed to 6 Dagmar Road, Camberwell, and died 5 March 1887, at the great age of 92 years.

Grave 4726 Sq 111. Headstone. **Sources:** LCC; MI; BC 1881; Elkington, George *The Worshipful Company of Coopers (not dated).*

CHARLES CLAUDE CARPENTER *CBE, D.Sc, JP, MICE,*
Knight of Grace of the Order of St John of Jerusalem **(1858-1938)**
Civil Engineer

Charles Claude Carpenter was born at Woolwich, Kent, on the 1 June 1858, a son of William Richard Carpenter RN. He was educated at Birkbeck College, and was appointed Engineer to the Vauxhall Gas Works in 1884. He was elected AMICE in 1886, a full member in 1896, and served as a member of the ICE Council from 1916 to 1924. He was President of the Institution of Gas Engineers in 1895.

In 1908, following the death of Sir George Thomas Livesey (q.v.), he became President of the South Metropolitan Gas Company. He was President of the Society of the Chemical Industry from 1915 to 1917, and served on the Chemical Warfare Committee and Munitions Inventions Panel, Ministry of Munitions, during World War I. He was appointed CBE for his war work in 1920, and received the degree of Doctor of Science from Leeds University.

Dr Carpenter resided at the 'White Lodge' Sandwich, Kent, and died at his London residence, 37 Cheyne Walk, Chelsea, on 7 September 1938, aged 80 years.

Grave 39817 Sq 52. Headstone. **Sources:** LCC; MI; *Journal of the Institution of Civil Engineers* Vol 10 (Obituary) 1938-39; KHB 1937; WW 1934; WWW Vol III.

ROBERT H. S. CARPENTER *LRCP, LSA* (1823-1890)
General Practitioner

Robert Carpenter was born in Bristol in 1823. He was for many years a general medical practitioner at 130 Stockwell Road, Lambeth. He died at his residence in Southampton Street (now Southampton Way) Camberwell, on 14 May 1890, aged 67 years.

The inscription on his gravestone reads: *This stone is erected by a few respectful and admiring medical friends of the deceased, who desire to show their appreciation of the unselfish manner in which he, during the greater part of his life, and at great personal cost and sacrifice of time, devoted his untiring energy and ability to promoting the interests of the general practitioners of the medical profession.'*

Grave 19915 Sq 8. Headstone. **Sources:** LCC; MI; BC 1881; *Medical directories.*

THOMAS CARTER (c1818-1867)
Military Writer and Historian

Thomas Carter was born about 1818, the son of William Carter of the Parish of St Sepulchres, London. He was employed for many years in the Adjutant General's Office, Horse Guards, Whitehall, having entered as a temporary clerk in 1839, and rising to the position of first class clerk. He assisted in the preparation of historical records of the army, and edited and published 'unofficial' records of the 26th and 44th regiments of foot.

Carter edited and published several works on military history including: *Curiosities of War and Military Studies* (1860), 2nd edition (1871), and *Medals of the British Army and How They Were Won* (1861). He was a regular contributor to 'Notes and Queries'. He died at his residence, 11 Lorrimore Square, Walworth, on 9 August 1867, aged 49 years.

Grave 2014 Squares 53-54. Headstone (damaged). **Sources:** LCC; MI; DNB; MEB Vol I 1892.

WILLIAM CHADWICK (1797-1852)
Stonemason, Architect, Engineer, Speculative Builder and Entrepreneur

William Chadwick was born at Pentonville on the 1 January 1797, the second son of John Chadwick (d.1821), mason. He commenced work as a stonemason at the age of 21, and rebuilt the pinnacles of St Saviour's Church (now Southwark Cathedral), and constructed the spire of Bow Church, Cheapside.

In 1823 he carried out work at Holy Trinity Church, Southwark, and built several houses in Trinity Church Square. He later executed the masonry work at St Peter's Church, Walworth, under the direction of Sir John Soane. Between 1832 and 1837 he was contracted to build the chapels and boundary walls at Kensal Green Cemetery by the General Cemetery Company.

Chadwick later turned his attention to railways and laid a line from Didcot to Oxford. He also built several bridges for the Great Western Railway. He became Chairman of the London and Richmond Railway Company. He worked on the construction of the Hippodrome Racecourse in North Kensington, and was involved in the speculative development of seven acres of the Ladbroke Estate, including building 114 houses and two pubs, namely the 'Prince Albert' in Kensington Park Road, and the 'Sun in Splendour' in Pembridge Road.

Chadwick owned a large portion of the Grove Park Estate at Camberwell which he acquired from Dr Lettsom. He died at his Camberwell residence on 5 December 1852, aged 55 years.

NB: A memorial to his memory was erected in Holy Trinity Church, Southwark. Chadwick Road, Peckham, which leads to his former estate at Grove Park, Camberwell, is named after him.

Grave 2330 Sq 70. Massive solid granite obelisk over brick vault at the highest point (200 feet above sea level) in Nunhead Cemetery. **Sources:** LCC; MI; MEB Vol I 1892; Blanch, William Harnett *Ye Parish of Camberwell* 1875 p 283; *Survey of London* XXV St George's Fields 1955; *Survey of London* XXXVII Northern Kensington 1973; Girouard, Mark *Victorian Pubs* 1975 p 38.

Colonel JOSEPH LEMUEL CHESTER LL.D, DCL, FRHisS (1821-1882)
American Genealogist

Joseph Lemuel Chester was born at Norwich, Connecticut on the 30 April 1821, the third son of Joseph Chester, a grocer, who died when Joseph Lemuel was 12-years-old. In 1838 he went to New York and found work as a clerk to a silk merchant, and spent his spare time writing and contributing articles and poems to various journals. In 1843 he published *Greenwood Cemetery and other Poems* under the pseudonym 'Julian Cramer'. In 1845 he went to Philadelphia and became Musical Editor of Godey's *Lady's Book*. In 1852 he became an editor of 'The Philadelphia Inquirer' and the 'Daily Sun'.

In 1854 he was elected a Member of the Philadelphia City Council, and in 1855 he was appointed aide-de-camp to the Governor of Philadelphia with the honorary military rank of colonel.

Chester left the USA for Britain in 1858, and after settling in London started researching the British origins of American families. A founder member of the Harleian Society, he was an indefatigable researcher and accomplished genealogist. In 1876 he published *The Registers of Westminster Abbey*, the result of ten years labour, and after his death he left behind 87 volumes of parish register extracts and 24 volumes of pedigree collections.

Colonel Chester resided in Bermondsey for the last twenty years of his life, and died at his residence, 124 Southwark Park Road, on 26 May 1882, aged 61 years.

NB: *A memorial to Colonel Chester was placed in Westminster Abbey by the Dean and Chapter.*

Grave 16816 Sq 90. Headstone/curbs. Sources: LCC; MI; British Census 1881; DNB; MEB Vol I 1892; Dean, John Ward *Memoir of Colonel Joseph L. Chester* 1887.

CHARLES HARTWELL HORNE CHEYNE MA, FRAS (1838-1877)
Astronomical Writer

Charles Hartwell Horne Cheyne was born in London on the 1 May 1838, the eldest son of the Revd Charles Cheyne, Second Master of Christ's Hospital. His maternal grandfather was the Revd Dr Thomas Hartwell Horne (q.v.). He was educated at the Merchant Taylors' School and St John's College, Cambridge. In 1863 he was appointed Second Mathematical Master at Westminster School.

Cheyne published a collection of *Algebraic Exercises* for use in public schools and was the author of *An Elementary Treatise on the Planetary Theory* (1862), and *The Earth's Motion of Rotation, including the theory of precession and nutation* (1867). He was elected FRAS in 1868. Poor health compelled him to remove to Devon in December 1876, and he died a few weeks later at 3 Avenue Cottages, Torquay, on New Years Day 1877.

Grave 5279 Sq 67. Brick grave. Sources: LCC; MI; MEB Vol I 1892; Royal Astronomical Society Monthly Notices Vol 37 (obit) February 1877.

Monument to Charles Goddard Clarke MP, JP. (collapsed and in ruins)
The tall granite column was blown down in the great wind storm in October 1987

Alderman CHARLES GODDARD CLARKE *JP, MP* (1849-1908)
Manufacturing Chemist and Politician

Charles Goddard Clarke was born at Aldersgate, London, on the 10 May 1849, the son of Richard Clarke of Peckham. He was educated at Liverpool, and became a partner in the famous firm of Potter and Clarke, wholesale druggists and manufacturing chemists of London and Manchester.

In 1873 he married Rebecca Potter, a daughter of Henry Potter, a prominent Peckham Baptist. Charles Clarke too, was a keen Baptist, and in 1874 he became a member of Spurgeon's Metropolitan Tabernacle, Newington.

He was also active in local politics, and served several years on the old Camberwell Parish Vestry. He was vice-chairman of several committees, including the Finance Committee in 1893-4. He also sat on the London County Council as the member for Peckham from 1898 to 1907. He was appointed an alderman in the newly created Metropolitan Borough of Camberwell in 1900, and served as the third Mayor of Camberwell in 1902-3.

A Liberal in politics, he unsuccessfully contested Dulwich in the General Election of 1895, and the Mile End Division of Tower Hamlets in 1900. He was eventually returned as the MP for the Peckham Division of Camberwell in 1906. Charles Goddard Clarke was Peckham's last Liberal MP, and died at his residence, South Lodge, Champion Hill, Camberwell, on 7 March 1908, aged 58 years.

Grave 16685 Sq 100. Grey granite column and urn *(in ruins having blown down in great wind storm October 1987).* **Sources:** LCC; MI; BC 1881 and 1891; *Vestry of Camberwell's 37th Annual Report 1892/3* 1893; KHB 1908; WWW Vol I; Jackson, W. Eric *Achievement - A Short History of the LCC* 1965 p 268; *Camberwell Official Guide* 1960; Beasley, John D. *Who Was Who in Peckham* 1985 pp 41-2.

JAMES CLEMENTS (1876-1955)
Former Secretary to the London Cemetery Company

James Clements was born on Boxing Day 1876. He joined the London Cemetery Company (owners of Highgate and Nunhead cemeteries) at the age of 14 in 1890, and was Secretary of the London Cemetery Company for nearly 40 of the 65 years he spent in its service.

Clements was appointed Secretary 'in absentia' while serving abroad with the armed forces during World War I. He took up the position soon after his demobilization in 1919, and retired in 1955. He was appointed Consultant to the Company for three years. He died at his residence, 32 Colyton Road, London, SE22, on 8 October 1955, aged 78 years.

Grave 43385 Sq 31. Headstone/curbs. Sources: LCC; MI; *Trades directories.*

CUTHBERT COLLINGWOOD *MA, MB, FLS, MRCP* (1826-1908)
Physician, Naturalist and Prominent Swedenborgian

Cuthbert Collingwood was born in Greenwich on Christmas Day 1826, the fifth son of Samuel Collingwood, architect, and Frances Collingwood, daughter of Samuel Collingwood, printer to the Oxford University. He was educated at King's College School, and Christ Church, Oxford, graduating BA in 1849, MA in 1852, and MB in 1854. His medical education was continued at Edinburgh University, Guys Hospital, London, and afterwards in Paris and Vienna.

A keen naturalist, Cuthbert Collingwood was elected FLS in 1853. From 1858 to 1866 he resided in Liverpool, and was Lecturer on Botany at the Royal Infirmary Medical School and Lecturer on Biology at the Liverpool School of Science. He was also Senior Physician to the Liverpool Northern Hospital.

In 1866 and 1867, he undertook, as a volunteer on board HMS *Rifleman* and *Serpent*, a scientific voyage for the study of marine zoology in the China Seas visiting Formosa, Borneo, Sarawak, Singapore, and the Phillipines. On his return to England he published *Rambles of a Naturalist on the Shores and Waters of the China Seas* (1868). He sat on the Council of the Linnean Society in 1868.

He was also the author of *The Travelling Birds* (1872), and numerous papers on natural history published in scientific journals. In 1876 he travelled to Egypt and Palestine and published an account of his journey.

Collingwood's family were Nonconformists. His mother's sister, Sophia Ann, was married to the Revd Dr Edward Bean Underhill, Secretary of the Baptist Missionary Society, and Collingwood was a prominent member of the New Jerusalem Church (Swedenborgian). He wrote several theological works in prose and verse including, *From Beyrout to Bethlehem*, *A Vision of Creation* (1882), *New Studies in Christian Theology* (1883), and *The Bible and the Age* (1886).

In 1869 Cuthbert Collingwood married Clara, the youngest daughter of Colonel Sir Robert Moubray of Cockairny House, near Aberdour, Fifeshire. She died in 1871.

In the 1880s Collingwood was living at Gipsy Hill, Lambeth, and resided in Paris from 1901 to 1906. He returned to England in 1907, and was living at 134 Ladywell Road, Lewisham in 1908. He died in Lewisham Infirmary on 20 October 1908, aged 81 years.

Grave 10106 Sq 116. Granite headstone. *Monumental mason: Alexander Nicholson, Mark Lane, London, EC.* **Sources:** LCC; MI; BC 1881; DNB; WWW Vol I; *Proceedings of the Linnean Society of London* 1909; Kirk, J. F. *Alibone's Dictionary of Authors Supplement* 1891; Plarr, Victor G. *Men and Women of the Time* 1899.

Revd Dr WILLIAM BENGO' COLLYER *DD, LL.D, FAS* (1782-1854)
Dissenting Divine

William Bengo' Collyer was born at Deptford on the 14 April 1782, the son of Thomas Collyer, builder. He was christened William Bengow at the Church of St Paul, Deptford, on the 12 May 1782. He was educated at the Leathersellers' Company School, Lewisham, and entered Homerton College when he was thirteen. He became a student of theology at the age of sixteen. In 1801 he was ordained Pastor of the Independent Chapel in the village of Peckham, Surrey.

Collyer, who called himself an English Presbyterian, was an able minister of the New Testament and his fame soon spread far and wide, eventually attracting the attention of the Dukes of Kent and Sussex, both of whom became his good friends. It was on the recommendation of the Duke of Kent that the 26-year-old Pastor received the Diploma of Doctor of Divinity from the University of Edinburgh in 1808.

In 1817 Peckham chapel was rebuilt and called 'Hanover Chapel' in recognition of its royal patronage.

Dr Collyer also preached at Salters' Hall Chapel, London from 1813 to 1825. He published numerous sermons, hymns and tracts. His first work *Fugitive Pieces for the use of Schools,* was issued in 1803. He also published seven volumes of lectures. The first, *Lectures on Scripture Facts* appeared in 1807. This was followed by *Lectures on Scripture Prophecy* (1809), *On Scripture Miracles* (1812), *On Scripture Parables* (1815), *On Scripture Doctrines* (1818), and *On Scripture Duties* (1820). The final volume, *Lectures of Scripture Comparison, or Christianity compared with Hinduism, Mohammedanism, the Ancient Philosophy and Deism,* was published in 1823. His last publication, *Hymns for Israel,* was issued in 1848. He died at Chislehurst, Kent, on 8 January 1854, aged 71 years.

Grave 1153 Sq 165. Chest tomb and urn over vault. Sources: LCC; MI; DNB; MEB Vol I 1892; *Congregational Year Book* 1855 pp 210 - 213; Waddington, John S*urrey Congregational History* 1866 pp 166-167, 265; Blanch, William Harnett *Ye Parish of Camberwell* 1875 pp 92, 186-7, 227, 231-232, 258, 283-5, 293, 298; *Allibone's Dictionary of Authors* 1877; Cleal, Edward E. *The Story of Congregationalism in Surrey* 1908.

Revd Dr WILLIAM COOKE *DD* (1806-1884)
Methodist New Connexion Minister

Dr Cooke was a Minister in the Methodist New Connexion from 1827 to death, and President of the New Connexion Conference in 1859. He was the author of *Christian Theology Explained and Defended* (1846), and several other works including a number of treatises on Roman Catholicism. He died at Burslem House, Park Road, Forest Hill, on Christmas Day 1884.
Grave *9479 Sq 145*. *Pedestal and urn*. Sources: LCC; MI; MEB Vol I 1892; Davey, Cyril J. *The Methodist Story* 1955 pp 65-6.

HENRY RAMSAY COX *FLS* (1844-1880)
Lepidopterist

The only son of Henry Cox of West Dulwich, Henry Ramsay Cox was an enthusiastic collector of butterflies, his name appearing frequently in the pages of *The Entomologist* and other scientific journals.

In 1857 he captured several Pale Clouded Yellow (Colias Hyale) near his home at Forest Hill. On a visit to Margate in the summer of 1868 he observed many thousands of the same species of butterfly at Marsh Bay. He wrote: 'It was a lovely sight to see these handsome creatures settled on the flowers and swaying to and fro in the wind; the rich gold of their underside contrasting beautifully with the purple flowers of the Lucerne.'

Cox was elected FLS in 1875 and died at 3 Tyson Road, Forest Hill, on 3 September 1880, aged 36 years.
Grave *472 Sq 125*. *Headstone*. Sources: LCC; MI; *Entomologist* 13 1880; *Zoologischer Anzeiger* Vol 3 1880; Newman, Edward, *The Natural History of British Butterflies* pp 142-3 1884; Letter from Miss Darell-Brown of the Linnean Society of London dated 29 January 1982.

PETER MILLER CUNNINGHAM *RN* (1789-1864)
Former Surgeon-Superintendent of Convict Ships

Peter Miller Cunningham was born at Dalwinton, Dumfrieshire, in November 1789, the fifth son of John Cunningham, farmer, friend and neighbour of the poet Robert Burns. His brothers, Allan Cunningham and Thomas Mounsey Cunningham were both well-known writers.

Peter Miller Cunningham was educated at the University of Edinburgh and became Assistant-Surgeon to the British Fleet off the coast of Spain in 1810, and Surgeon RN in 1814. After 1818 he made four voyages to New South Wales, as Surgeon-Superintendent of Convict Ships. His first voyage was in 1819 on board the transport *Recovery*. His proud boast was that 600 felons were safely transported under his care without the loss of a single life. Robert Hughes

(*The Fatal Shore*) claims that Cunningham made at least five voyages to Australia as Surgeon-Superintendent on convict transports and lost only three of the 747 convicts under his care.

He was the author of *Two Years in New South Wales; comprising sketches of the actual state of society in that colony; of its peculiar advantages to emigrants; of its topography, natural history, etc.* 2 vols 1827, and *Hints for Australian Emigrants* 1841. An account of his visit to the Falkland Islands appeared in the *Athenaeum*. Peter Cunningham left the sea in 1841 and spent the last years of his life at Greenwich. He died at 11 Lovegrove Place, Greenwich on 6 May 1864, aged 74 years.

Grave 7992 Sq 126. Headstone. Sources: LCC; MI; DNB; MEB Vol I 1892; Hughes, Robert *The Fatal Shore - A History of The Transportation of Convicts to Australia 1787-1868* Folio Society Edition 1998.

JOHN SPARKS DALTON (1816-1852)
Banker and Journalist

John Sparks Dalton was born on 8 November 1816. A contributor to numerous publications on banking he was the founder and first editor of *The Bankers Magazine*. He died at No 6 Southampton Street, Strand on Christmas Eve 1852, aged 36 years. The pedestal monument over his grave bears the following inscription: *'Erected by his many banking friends in appreciation of the valuable services he rendered to the banking community'*

Grave 2041 Sq 96. Pedestal. Sources: LCC; MI; *Trades directories*.

Sir POLYDORE DE KEYSER *JP, FRGS, FSS* etc (1832-1897)
First Roman Catholic Lord Mayor of London since the Reformation

A naturalised Briton, Polydore De Keyser was born at Termonde, Belgium, on the 13 December 1832, the son of Constant De Keyser of Antwerp. After working for many years in his father's London restaurant, he built a magnificent hotel overlooking the Thames. Opened by the King of the Belgians in 1874, De Keyser's Royal Hotel at Blackfriars was the largest establishment of its kind in London.

De Keyser took an active interest in politics becoming an Alderman for Farringdon Without and Sheriff of London in 1882. He overcame bigoted opposition in 1887 to become the first Roman Catholic Lord Mayor of London since the Reformation.

He was a guest of the King of the Belgians at the Royal Palace in Brussels in February 1888, and made a state visit to Termonde, his birth-place, in August 1888. He was knighted at Windsor Castle on 4 December 1888, and was President of the British Section of the Paris Exhibition in 1889. A past master of several City livery companies, Sir Polydore was also a generous supporter of a large number of charities.

He resided several years at Chatham House, Grove Road, Clapham Park and died at No 4 Cornwall Mansions, South Kensington, on 14 January 1897, aged 64 years.

Grave 22321 Sq 148. Large cross over brick vault. **Sources:** LCC; MI; British Census 1881; MEB Vol V 1912; KHB 1895; WWW Vol I; Fox-Davies A. C. *Armorial Families* 1893; Smith, Eric E. E. *Clapham - An Historical Tour* 1975; Taylor D. and Bush D. *The Golden Age of British Hotels* 1974.

WILLIAM LUCAS DISTANT *FES* (1845-1922)
Naturalist and Editor of 'Zoologist' 1897-1915

William Lucas Distant was born in Rotherhithe on the 12 November 1845, the son of Captain Alexander Distant, master mariner. He was educated privately, and became an all round naturalist.

Distant was Director and Honorary Secretary of the Anthropological Institute from 1878 to 1881; Secretary of the Entomological Society from 1878 to 1880; and Vice-President of the Entomological Society in 1881 and 1900.

He spent some time abroad and made natural history collections in the Malay Peninsular and the Transvaal. He published numerous works on entomology, lepidoptera and coleoptera, and some on anthropology. He was the editor of *Zoologist* from 1897 to 1915.

Distant resided several years at 'Glenside', Birchanger Road, South Norwood, and died at Cornwall House (Nursing Home), Grove Road, Wanstead, Essex, on 4 February 1922, aged 76 years.

Grave 9394 Sq 53. Headstone. **Sources:** LCC; MI; British Census 1881; WWW Vol II.

JOHN DIXON *MD, CM, MRCS, LRCP, JP* (1832-1930)
Physician and Amateur Historian

John Dixon was born at Magby, the son of John Dixon of Hessle, Yorkshire. He was educated at St Andrews University, and on qualifying as surgeon and physician he opened a general practise in Grange Road, Bermondsey. He was also Medical Officer of Health for Bermondsey. In 1872 he sold his practise to David Smart (q.v.).

Dr Dixon was a local historian and the author of *The Chronicles of Bermondsey.* He was a popular lecturer on the ancient history of Bermondsey,

and a local magistrate. He died at his residence, 133 Jamaica Road, Bermondsey, on 30 March 1930, at the advanced age of 97 years.
Grave 23202 Sq 70. Headstone. **Sources:** LCC; MI; BC 1881; KHB; Clarke, Edward T. *Bermondsey* 1902 p 252.

BRYAN DONKIN *FRS, MRAS* (1768-1855)
Civil Engineer and Inventor

Bryan Donkin was born at Fountain Hall, Sandoe, Northumberland, on the 22 March 1768. In 1792 he was apprenticed to John Hall, a Dartford millwright, who later became his brother-in-law. In 1803 he began working at a small engineering works in Bermondsey financed by the Fourdrinier Brothers, and in partnership with them invented a paper making machine and a composition printing roller.

Donkin patented numerous inventions including the first practical steel pen nib as an alternative to the quill. In 1810 he received a gold medal from the Society of Arts for his mercury tachometer which was used for measuring the speed of machines. He is best known however, for devising a method of preserving meat in air-tight metal containers in 1812, and built a large food canning factory in Bermondsey. In 1823 he became a Director of the new Thames Tunnel Company and Marc Brunel was appointed Engineer.

A founder Member of the Institution of Civil Engineers, Bryan Donkin was elected FRS in 1838. He was a Member of the Royal Astronomical Society and built a small observatory in his garden.

He died at his residence, 6 The Paragon, New Kent Road, on 27 February 1855, aged 86 years.

Grave 126 Sq 68. Granite ledger over brick vault. **Sources:** LCC; MI; Information from Institution of Civil Engineers; DNB; MEB Vol I 1892; Bryan Donkin & Co. *A Brief Account of Bryan Donkin FRS and the Company he Founded* (nd); Miller, Harry *Hall's of Dartford 1785-1985* 1985 pp 27-30, 32, 33, 43; Vaughan, Adrian *I. K. Brunel - Engineering Knight Errant* 1991 p 13.

BRYAN DONKIN *MICE* (1809-1893)
Civil and Mechanical Engineer

Bryan Donkin was born in Southwark on the 29 April 1809, the fifth son of Bryan Donkin FRS (q.v.). He was educated at Bromley, Kent, and in London and Paris. After leaving school he entered his father's works and became a senior partner in the firm. In 1829 he was sent to France to supervise the construction of paper milling machinery at Nantes. He was in France during the revolution of 1830. On returning home he joined his brothers as a partner at the family's Bermondsey works. He took out several patents for paper-making machinery alone and with Barnard William Farey (q.v.).

In 1858 he was contracted to build a paper mill at St Petersburg for the manufacture of banknotes. The mill was completed in 1862 and he received the personal thanks of the Czar of Russia. Donkin retired in 1881 and died at his residence, Eastnor House, 1 Lloyds Place, Blackheath, on 4 December 1893.

Grave 126A Sq 68. Red granite pedestal over vault. *Monument erected by his son Bryan Donkin.* **Sources:** LCC; MI; BC 1881; MEB Vol V 1912; *Institution of Civil Engineers Minutes of Proceedings* Vol 15.

Sir HORATIO BRYAN DONKIN *MD, MA, FRCP, MRCS* (1845-1927)
Physician and Criminologist

Horatio Bryan Donkin was born at Charlton, Kent on 4 February 1845, the eldest son of Bryan Donkin MICE (q.v.), and grandson of Bryan Donkin FRS (q.v.). He was educated at Blackheath Proprietary School and Queen's College, Oxford.

Horatio Donkin was Physician and Lecturer on Medicine at Westminster Hospital; Lecturer on Medicine at the London School of Medicine for Women; and Examiner for Medicine at the Royal College of Physicians. He was HM Commissioner of Prisons for England and Wales from 1898 to 1910, and Medical Adviser to the Prison Commission from 1910 to 1915.

He was a Director of Convict Prisons and a prominent member of the Society for the Prevention of Venereal Disease. He published numerous papers including several on mental pathology and crime. He was knighted in 1911, and died at 28 Hyde Park Street, Paddington, on 26 July 1927, aged 82 years.

Grave 126B Sq 68. Headstone over vault. **Sources:** LCC; MI; BC 1881; KHB; WWW Vol II.

Sir STANFORD EDWIN DOWNING *BA, LL.B* (1870-1933)
Barrister and Civil Servant

Stanford Edwin Downing was born in Camberwell on the 21 January 1870, the son of Henry Downing of Boyton, Cornwall, and a younger brother of Henry

Philip Burke Downing FSA, church architect. He was educated at Wilson's Grammar School, Camberwell, and at the University of London.

Downing entered the Ecclesiastical Commission in 1892, and was called to the Bar at Lincoln's Inn in 1903. He was appointed Secretary to the Ecclesiastical and Church Estates Commissioners in 1910. He became Financial Adviser to the Ecclesiastical Commission in 1922, and was knighted in 1926. He died suddenly at Wimbledon on 12 June 1933, aged 63 years.

Grave No 14591 Sq 84. Large granite cross on stepped base (ruins). **Sources:** LCC: MI; BC 1881; WWW Vol III; Allport, D. H. *A Short History of Wilson's Grammar School* 1964 pp 195, 210, 214, 227.

Revd ANDREW AUGUSTUS WILD DREW *MA* (1837-1921)
Anglican Priest

Andrew Augustus Wild Drew was born at Woodstock, Canada, on the 5 June 1837, the second son of Admiral Andrew Drew RN. He was brother-in-law to Admiral Sir Algernon Frederick Rous de Horsey.

Andrew A. W. Drew was educated at Trinity College, Cambridge, and took orders in 1860. He was successively Curate of Benenden, Kent; Ewhurst, Sussex; and Christ Church, Forest Hill; before founding the Mission of St Michael and All Angels at Linden Grove, Nunhead, in 1865. The mission church was replaced by St Antholin's Parish Church, Nunhead in 1878. Mr Drew was appointed the first vicar.

He ministered at Nunhead for over 45 years retiring in 1911 at the age of 75 years. He died at North Road House, Clapham, on 13 October 1921.

Grave 21052 Sq 51. Headstone. **Sources:** LCC; MI; Crockford; Blanch, William Harnett *Ye Parish of Camberwell* 1875 p 222; Smith, Roger (ed) *Centenary Viewpoint - St Antony's Nunhead 1878-1978* 1978.

Revd GEORGE SMITH DREW *MA, FRGS* (1818-1880)
Anglican Priest and Author

George Smith Drew was born at Louth, Lincolnshire on 13 June 1818, the son of George Drew, a London tea dealer. He took orders in 1843 and was Vicar of St John the Evangelist, St Pancras from 1850 to 1854; Vicar of Pulloxhill, Bedfordshire from 1854 to 1858; Vicar of St Barnabas, South Kensington from 1858 to 1870; and Rector of Avington, Hampshire from 1870 to 1872. He was Hulsean Lecturer at Cambridge in 1877, and was Vicar of Holy Trinity,

Lambeth from 1872 to his death which occurred at Holy Trinity Vicarage on 21 January 1880. George Drew made a tour of the East in 1856 and was elected FRGS. He was the author of at least 14 works on religious subjects including, *Sermons* (1845), *Scripture Studies in the Old Testament* (1855), and *Scripture Lands in Connection with their History* (1860).

Grave 15691 Sq 68. Tomb over vault. **Sources:** LCC; MI; DNB; MEB Vol I 1892; *Alumni Canta.*

AUGUSTUS EDWARD DURANDEAU (1848-1893)
Composer of Music Hall Songs

Augustus Edward Durandeau was born in Liverpool in 1848. He described himself as a Professor of Music in 1881 at which time he was living with his American wife Mary at No 185 Beresford Street, Walworth. His many compositions include the coster song, *Never introduce your donah (girlfriend) to a pal,* made famous by Gus Elen, and *Stop the cab.* In collaboration with Edward W. Rogers he wrote *Come where the booze is cheaper,* sung 'with immense success' by Charles Coburn, and *If you want to know the time ask a policeman,* an amusing song popularised by the red-nosed comedian James Fawn.

Durandeau died at 10 Beresford Buildings, Walworth, on 26 February 1893, aged 44 years. He is buried in a common grave with 19 other poor folk.

Grave 21367 Sq 58. Unmarked grave. **Sources:** LCC; BC 1881; MEB Vol V 1912; Baker, Richard Anthony *Marie Lloyd - Queen of the Music-halls* 1990 pp 22 and 148; Batten, Rex *Nunhead and the Music Hall - A Guide to Music Hall Personalities in Nunhead Cemetery* 2000.

BENJAMIN EDGINGTON (1794-1869)
Marquee Maker to HM Queen Victoria

Benjamin Edgington was born at Abingdon, Berkshire, on 4 September 1794. In 1823 he founded his business making tents and tarpaulins at No 5 Tooley Street (at the foot of old London Bridge) and remained there until 1835. Having acquired premises in the City of London and in the West End, he became the largest tent and marquee maker in England, supplying the War Office, the Admiralty, and HM Queen Victoria.

He was the sole manufacturer of *Captain Wetherest's* convertible hammock and travelling tent, which won a prize medal at the Great Exhibition in 1851. He died at his residence, The Elms, Upper Tooting, on 29 August 1869, leaving behind him a personal fortune of £120,000. A company bearing his name existed in the 1950s.

Grave 10313 Sq 94. Tomb over vault. **Sources:** LCC; MI; MEB Vol 1892; *Trades directories.*

GEORGE ELKINGTON *FRIBA* (1824-1897)
Architect and Surveyor

George Elkington was born in Bermondsey and educated at King's College School, London. He was articled to George Porter and later opened his own office in London where he practised from 1847 until his retirement in 1895. He was elected FRIBA in 1854, and was transferred to the class of Retired Fellows in 1895.

Elkington was appointed Surveyor to the Vestry of Bermondsey in 1855. He designed buildings at Epsom Medical College (1862), and carried out work to Bermondsey Workhouse. He was in partnership with his son from 1875 to 1895. The Elkingtons designed Lewisham Town Hall (1876); Penge Vestry Hall (1879); and Bermondsey Vestry Hall (1882). Other works carried out by the partnership include Rotherhithe Public Baths, Richmond Public Baths, a Congregational Church at Anerley, the London Leather Centre in Bermondsey, and Coborn School, Bow.

George Elkington was Under Warden of the Coopers Company in 1870, and Master of the Coopers Company in 1885 and 1886. He lived many years at Briarford, Anerley Road, Penge, before removing to Worthing in 1895. He died at 139 Oakdene, Victoria Road, Worthing, Sussex, on 23 July 1897, aged 73 years.

Grave 19219 Sq 139. Obelisk *in ruins. (bomb damage in World War II).*
Sources: LCC; MI; British Census 1881; Pevsner, N. *Buildings of England - London* Vol 2; RIBA Journal Vol 4, (obituary) 1897 pp 438-9; Cunningham, Colin *Victorian & Edwardian Town Halls* 1981 pp 103, 277, 281, 247.

BARNARD WILLIAM FAREY *MICE* (1827-88)
Civil Engineer and Inventor

Barnard William Farey was born at Lambeth on 12 August 1827. Farey's father died when he was nine years old and he was sent to Nantes, France where his uncle Monsieur Colomb Gengembre was a civil engineer.

Farey was trained by his uncle, and was later employed at the Marine Engine and Ship-building Works of the French Government at Indret. He resigned his post aged sixteen and returned to England, continuing his technical education in London. He worked at the Fairfield Works, Bow before joining Bryan Donkin and Sons in 1847, eventually becoming a partner in the firm. He designed the first gas valve with internal rack and pinion for the Gas-Light and Coke Company in 1847, and invented a double cylinder rag boiler for paper makers in 1849. He took out several patents for steam machinery over a period of twenty-one years. He was elected MICE in 1865.

Barnard Farey died at his residence, Salamanca, Farquhar Road, Dulwich, on 9 May 1888, aged 60 years.

Grave 19149 Sq 70. Granite chest tomb. **Sources:** LCC; MI; BC 1881; Institution of Civil Engineers - Minutes of Proceedings (Obituary) Vol 94; MEB (mentioned in the entry for Bryan Donkin).

Sir ANTHONY FELL (1914-1998)
Former Conservative MP for Great Yarmouth 1951-66 and 1970-83

Anthony Fell was born on the 18 May 1914, the son of Commander David Mark Fell RN. He was educated at Bedford Grammar School and in New Zealand. He was Conservative MP for Norfolk (Yarmouth Division) from 1951 to 1966 when he was defeated by the Labour candidate Hugh Gray, and MP for Great Yarmouth from 1970 to 1983. He was knighted in 1982.

Fell was against joining the Common Market; in the House of Commons, in 1961, he made his position clear. He referred to the Prime Minister Harold Macmillan, who was intent in leading Britain into Europe, as a 'national disaster'. 'His (Mr Macmillan's) decision to gamble with British Sovereignty, and with 650 million people in the British Commonwealth, is the most disastrous thing any Prime Minister has done for many generations past,' asserted the 'ferocious' Member for Great Yarmouth. He also called for the Prime Minister's resignation.

Sir Anthony was a Member of Parliament for for 28 years. He died at 11 Denny Street, Kennington, London, SE11, in March 1998, aged 83 years.

Grave No 46146 Sq 17. Small cross. **Sources:** Burial Records; MI; KHB; WW 1987; *Whitaker's Almanack* 1980; *Guardian Century 1960-1969* 1999; Information from Mrs Michele Louise Burford.

HENRY WILLIAM FIELD (1803-1888)
Queen's Assaymaster & Descendant of Oliver Cromwell

Henry Field was a lineal descendant of Oliver Cromwell, Lord Protector of the Commonwealth. He was born at Hammersmith on the 23 March 1803, the fourth son of John Field (1764-1845), Umpire of the Royal Mint. He entered the Royal Mint at the age of 15 and became probationer assayer in 1836.

Field exhibited eight designs for coins at the Royal Academy from 1822 to 1827, and was appointed HM Queen's Assaymaster at the Royal Mint in 1851. While working at the Mint he made chemically pure gold and brought the coin of the realm up to mathematical perfection.

He was married to Anne, daughter of the Revd Thomas Mills. She died in 1868. He retired from the Royal Mint in 1871, and resided for several years at Munster Lodge, Broom Road, Teddington, Surrey. He died at No 10 Chesham Place, Brighton, Sussex, on 9 June 1888, aged 85 years.

Grave 3652 Sqs 78-79. Headstone. **Sources:** LCC; MI; BC 1881; MEB Vol I 1892.

*Figgins monument
(restored 2001)*

JAMES FIGGINS *JP* (1811-1884)
City of London Typefounder. Former MP for Shrewsbury

James Figgins was born in the Parish of St Sepulchres, London, on the 16 April 1811, the second son of Vincent Figgins (q.v.). He was educated by Dr Brown of Esher, and afterwards joined his father's firm as a letter founder at West Street, Smithfield. James and his elder brother Vincent II (q.v.) took over their father's foundry in 1836 and traded as V & J Figgins.

James Figgins took an active interest in City affairs, and was Sheriff of London and Middlesex 1865-6. He was an Alderman for Farringdon Without from 1873 to 1882, and one of Queen Victoria's Lieutenants for the City of London. He was a JP for Middlesex.

A Conservative in politics, Figgins was Member of Parliament for Shrewsbury from 1868 to 1874. He died at his London residence, 35 Russell Square, Bloomsbury, on 12 June 1884, aged 73 years.

Grave 248 Sq 68. *Neo-classical canopied tomb* over brick vault signed: *W. P. Griffiths, architect; John Mallcott, sculptor; and Henry Daniel, stonemason.* Listed Grade II 1998. **Sources:** LCC; MI; *Debrett's House of Commons and the Judicial Bench* 1872; BC 1881; MEB Vol I 1892.

VINCENT FIGGINS (c1767-1844)
City of London Typefounder

Vincent Figgins was born c1767. He was apprenticed to Joseph Jackson, a letter founder, at the age of fifteen, and worked with his master until the latter's death in 1792.

Figgins established his own foundry at White Swan Yard, Holborn Bridge, in 1792 removing to 17 West Street, Smithfield, in 1802. He published his *Type Specimens* in 1801 and 1815. When he retired in 1836 he handed over the running of the business to his two sons, Vincent Figgins II (q.v.), and James Figgins (q.v.). He devoted the remaining years of his life to his work as a Common Councillor in the City of London.

He died at his country residence, 1 Prospect Place, Peckham Rye, on 29 February 1844, aged 76 years.

NB: (1) Frederic Boase, *Modern English Biography*, confuses Vincent Figgins with his son Vincent Figgins II, and gives his date of death incorrectly as December 1860 or January 1861. (2) *Vincent Figgins, Type Specimens 1801 & 1815* was reproduced in facsimile by the Printing Historical Society in 1967, edited with introduction and notes by Berthold Wolpe.

Grave 248 Sq 68. tomb. Sources: LCC; MI; MEB Vol I 1892 (entry for James Figgins); Dowding, Geoffrey *An Introduction to the History of Printing Types* 1961; Todd W. B. *Directory of Printers and Others in Allied Trades, London & Vicinity* 1972.

VINCENT FIGGINS II (1807-1860)
City of London Typefounder

The eldest son of Vincent Figgins (q.v.), Vincent junior trained as a letter founder in his father's foundry, and in 1836 he became a partner with his brother James Figgins (q.v.) at the West Street Foundry, Smithfield. In 1859, the year before his untimely death at the early age of 53, he published a facsimile edition of Caxton's book *The Game and the Playe of the Chesse*.

He resided at Southgate, Middlesex, and died at Nice (then in Italy) on 21 December 1860. His body was brought back to England and was placed in the family vault in Nunhead Cemetery in January 1861. NB: A memorial window was erected in the Church of Christ Church, Southgate, inscribed: 'In memory of Vincent Figgins, who died Decr. XXI., MDCCCLX., aged LIII. By his affectionate wife Rosanna.'

Grave No 248 Square 68. Tomb over vault. Sources: LCC; MI; Cansick, Frederick Teague *Cansick's Epitaphs of Middlesex* 1875 page xvi; Todd, W. B. *Directory of Printers and Others in Allied Trades, London & Vicinity* 1972.

Surgeon-Major JOHN FINDLAY *MB, CM, CIE* (1851-1920)
Former Surgeon to the Viceroy of India

John Findlay was born in Ayr, Scotland, on the 29 July 1851. He received his medical education at Edinburgh University and joined the Army Medical Staff as surgeon in 1875. He served as a Medical Officer in the second Afghan War and Burma Campaign, and was Surgeon to the Governor of Bombay from 1881 to 1884. He was Surgeon to the Viceroy of India from 1884 to 1888. Findlay was promoted to the rank of Surgeon-Major in 1889 and appointed CIE. He died at 43 Jermyn Street, London W1, on 14 January 1920.

Grave 33762 Sq 89. Art Deco headstone/cross. Sources: LCC; MI; KHB; WWW Vol II 1929; Johnson, W. *Commissioned Officers in the Medical Service of the Army 1660-1960* 1968.

Sir CHARLES FOX *MICE, FSA* (1810-1874)
Civil Engineer: Contractor for the Crystal Palace

Charles Fox was born at Derby on 11 March 1810 the fourth and youngest son of Dr Francis Fox MD. At the age of 19 he was apprenticed to the Swedish engineer Captain Ericcson and assisted with the construction of the *Novelty* locomotive.

From 1830 to 1835 he was employed by Robert Stephenson as Assistant Constructing Engineer to the London and Birmingham Railway. He designed the Watford tunnel and constructed a line from Camden Town to Euston. He also introduced the switch into railway practise.

After 1840 Charles Fox ran his own business. His most ambitious undertaking was to construct Paxton's Crystal Palace at Hyde Park for the Great Exhibition of 1851. He began working on the project in the autumn of 1850 and completed the work at the end of April 1851. He personally worked for eighteen hours a day for seven weeks to ensure the building was ready in time.

On Saturday 28 June 1851 he was entertained by his fellow townsmen at a public dinner which took place at the Royal Hotel, Derby. He was knighted, together with Sir Joseph Paxton and Sir William Cubitt, on the 23 October 1851.

In 1854 Sir Charles was contracted to rebuild the great glass and metal building on the heights of Sydenham, and there it remained until it was destroyed by fire in 1936.

Other works by Sir Charles as manufacturer and contractor include bridges over the Thames and Medway, railway lines at Battersea for the London & Brighton & Chatham & Dover Railway Companies, and the Berlin Waterworks. From 1857 onwards he practised in London as a Civil and Consulting Engineer in partnership with his two elder sons. He died at Blackheath on 14 June 1874, aged 64 years.

Grave 12861 Sq 67. Granite tomb over brick grave. Sources: LCC: MI; DNB; MEB Vol I 1892; 'The Illustrated London News' 5 July 1851 pp 21-22; Walford, Edward *The County Families of the United Kingdom* 1860; Institution of Civil Engineers - Minutes of Proceedings Vol 39; Beaver, Patrick *The Crystal Palace* 1970; Bird, Anthony *Paxton's Palace* 1976.

Lieutenant-Colonel FRANCIS FULLER CB (1791-1853)
Veteran of Waterloo and the Peninsular War

Francis Fuller was born in 1791, the eldest son of Lieut-General Francis Fuller. In 1806 he joined the 59th (2nd Nottinghamshire) Regiment of Foot with the rank of Ensign. He served with his regiment at the capture of the Cape Good Hope; Battle of Vittoria; the Siege of San Sebastian; the Battle of the Nive, where he was wounded; the Battle of Waterloo; the storming of Cambray; and the capture of Paris. He afterwards proceeded to India where he commanded his regiment at the siege and capture of Bhurtpore in 1825-6.

Fuller was made CB in 1826. He was promoted to the rank of Lieutenant Colonel in 1828, and sold his commission in 1834. He died at 6 Edgerton Road, Greenwich, on 27 May 1853, aged 62 years.

NB: Charles Dalton, compiler of *The Waterloo Roll Call* published 1904, states incorrectly that Colonel Fuller died in Jersey in 1868.

Grave 2462 Sq 107. Headstone (faded inscription). **Sources:** LCC; MI; MEB Vol V 1912; 'Gentleman's Magazine' July 1853; Dalton, Charles *The Waterloo Roll Call* 1904.

CHARLES GANDON *MICE* (1837-1902)
Civil Engineer: President of the Society of Gas Engineers 1885

Charles Gandon was born on 13 June 1837 and began his engineering career as a pupil of Henry Palfrey Stephenson. In 1861 he became Assistant Engineer to the Great Northern Railway Company, and by 1863 he was Manager and Engineer to the Ottoman Gas Company in Turkey, where he superintended the erection of the Smyrna Gas Works.

In 1869 Gandon was Manager and Engineer to the Bombay Gas Works, and three years later he was working in South America, where he was in charge of the Para Gas Works in Brazil. On returning to England, he was appointed Engineer to the Crystal Palace Gas Company in 1876. He was President of the Society of Gas Engineers in 1885, and President of the Gas Institute in 1888. Gandon retired in 1897 but continued to serve on the boards of several gas companies. He died at his residence, The Woodlands, Tressillian Road, Brockley on 8 October 1902, aged 65 years.

Grave 26561 Sq 70. Cross on stepped base. **Sources:** LCC; MI; Institution of Civil Engineers - Minutes of Proceedings (obit) Vol 151; Information from the Institution of Civil Engineers.

Commander EDWARD GARRETT *RN* (1792-1882)
Royal Naval Officer

Edward Garrett was born at Broadhamston, Devon, in 1792. He entered the Navy at the age of 14 as Midshipman on board HMS *Explosion* in October 1806. He was wrecked off Heligoland in September 1807. He later served on board HMS *Grampus* in the China Seas, and was attached to HMS *Royal Oak*, flagship of Sir Pulteney Malcolm in 1812. As Master's Mate in charge of a tender, Mr Garrett co-operated in the attack upon New Orleans in 1814. He was promoted to the rank of Lieutenant in 1815, and given command of the *Express* cutter. He rose to the rank of Commander and died at No 51 Camden Grove, Peckham, on 5 February 1882, aged 90 years.

Grave 4636 Sq 46. Headstone. **Sources:** LCC; MI; BC 1881; O'Byrne, W. R. *A Naval Biographical Dictionary* 1849.

Mrs LINA GILLIGAN (1837-1911)
Schoolteacher: Grandmother to the Cricketing Gilligan Brothers

Mrs Emmeline Sophia Caroline Elizabeth Gilligan, aka Lina Gilligan, was born in Hanover, Germany. She was married to James William Gilligan of Clapton, and for many years ran a private school in Camberwell Grove.

Mrs Gilligan was grandmother to three first class cricketers namely: Frank William Gilligan OBE (1893-1960), who played for Essex; Arthur Edward Robert Gilligan (1894-1976), a noted Captain of England who played for both Surrey and Sussex; and Alfred Herbert Harold Gilligan (1896-1978), a Sussex cricketer who captained England in 1929/30. Mrs Gilligan died at 45 Grove Hill Road, Camberwell, on 29 September 1911, aged 74 years.

Grave 20393 Sq 25. Small monument (in ruins). **Sources:** LCC; MI; BC 1881.

HAROLD JAMES GLANVILLE *JP* (1854-1930)
Liberal MP for Bermondsey from 1910 to 1922

Harold James Glanville was born in Bermondsey on the 5 June 1854, the only son of James Glanville of Hatcham, chartered accountant. He was educated at Deptford Grammar School and was employed by the GPO before joining his father's firm. In 1883 he entered into partnership with his father-in-law, James Abbott, and became head of James White Abbott & Company (Mill Finishers) of Bermondsey.

Glanville took an active interest in local and public affairs, and served as the LCC Member (Progressive) for Rotherhithe from 1898 to 1910. He was MP (Liberal) for Southwark, Bermondsey from 1910 to 1918, and for Bermondsey West from 1918 to 1922. He died at his residence, Westwood, Sydenham, London, SE26 on 27 September 1930, aged 76 years. NB: His eldest son Harold Glanville was President of the Liberal Party 1959-1960.

Grave 18318 Sq 75. Headstone. **Sources:** LCC; MI; BC 1881; KHB; WWW Vol III; Jackson, W. E. *Achievement - A Short History of the LCC* 1965.

THOMAS GODDARD *RN* (1770-1853)
Purser and Paymaster of HM Royal Yacht

Thomas Goddard spent 68 years in the Royal Navy, during which time he was for over 30 years Purser and Paymaster of HM Royal Yacht *Royal George*. He died at his residence, No 1 Waterfield Terrace, Shooters Hill Road, Blackheath, 29 March 1853, aged 83 years.

Grave 29 Square 96. Railed tomb. **Sources:** LCC; MI; Rhind, Neil *Blackheath Village & Environs 1790-1970* Vol 2 1983 p 403.

Field Marshal Sir **WILLIAM MAYNARD GOMM** *GCB, DCL, LL.D*
(1784-1875) *Veteran of Waterloo*

William Maynard Gomm was born in Barbados on the 10 November 1784, the eldest son of Lieut-Colonel William Gomm of the 46th Regiment. He entered the army as Ensign at the age of 10, and at the age of 14 carried the colours of the 9th Regiment of Foot - the Holy Boys - into action in Holland.

He served in the Peninsular Campaign from 1810 to 1814, and was present at the battles of Quatre Bras and Waterloo in 1815. He was Commander in Jamaica from 1839 to 1842; Governor of Mauritius from 1842 to 1849; and Commander-in-Chief in India from 1850 to 1855. He was promoted Field Marshal in 1868, and was Constable of the Tower of London from 1872 to death.

Sir William, who had been Lord of the Manor of Rotherhithe since 1822, gave the land on which Christ Church and All Saints' Church, Rotherhithe, were built.

He died at Brighton, Sussex, in March 1875, and was buried in his family grave at Christ Church, Rotherhithe. The church was demolished to make way for road widening improvements in the late 1970s, and Sir William's remains and those of his wife were exhumed and buried in Nunhead Cemetery on the 26 November 1979.

Grave 44795 Sq 32. Small modern headstone. **Sources:** Nunhead Cemetery Burial Records; DNB; MEB Vol I 1892; Dalton, Charles *The Waterloo Roll Call* 1904; Information supplied by Mr Lou Hedger, Superintendent of Southwark Cemeteries in 1982.

FREDERICK GORRINGE (1831-1909)
Founder of Gorringe's Department Store, Belgravia

Frederick Gorringe was born on the 30 June 1831, the son of Pennington Gorringe II, and brought up on his uncle's farm near Eastbourne, Sussex. In 1858 he went to London and opened a small drapery shop in Buckingham Palace Road, Belgravia. His business, patronized by the nobility and gentry, prospered and expanded, and by 1869 occupied three shop premises.

In the early years of the 20th century a large department store replaced the small row of shops, and occupied the entire street frontage in Buckingham Palace Road from Brewer Street to Princes Street. Built between 1905 and 1908, Frederick Gorringe's Emporium was one of the most fashionable department stores in London's west-end. It survived well into the 1960s.

Frederick Gorringe died at his residence No 7 Victoria Road, Clapham on 10 April 1909, aged 77 years.

Grave 14519 Sq 67. Large white marble cross (broken). **Sources:** LCC; MI; Adburgham, A. *Shops and Shopping 1800-1914* 1981; *Trades directories.*

Captain **WILLIAM GOULD** *RN* **(1790-1866)**
Officer in the Royal Navy

William Gould was born on the 4 September 1790. He entered the Navy on the 31 March 1805, aged 14 years, as first class volunteer on board HM Frigate *Endymion*, assisting at the siege and evacuation of the strong Neapolitan fortress of Gaeta in July 1806. He removed to HMS *Seahorse* in the summer of 1806.

In 1808 Mr Gould joined HMS *Liberty* bound for the West Indies, and took part in the capture of the *Marie-Galante*. He also commanded a boat in an unsuccessful attempt to cut out a French corvette. In HMS *Neptune* he contributed to the reduction of Martinique, and was promoted to the rank of Lieutenant.

In 1830 he served at Salisbury as a Special Constable during the riots, and was recommended to the Government for the active part he took in their suppression. In 1834 he was appointed to the Coast Guard. Captain Gould died in Peckham on 6 January 1866, aged 75 years.

Grave 4714 Sq 143. Headstone. Sources: LCC; MI; O'Byrne, W. R. *A Naval Biographical Dictionary* 1849.

WILLIAM SUTTON GOVER *FSS, FIA* (1822-1894)
Founder of the British Equitable Assurance Company

William Sutton Gover was born in the Old Kent Road on the 17 November 1822, the son of William Gover of Havering House, Blackheath. He was Secretary and Actuary to the British Empire Mutual Life Assurance Company before founding the British Equitable Assurance Company at No 47 King William Street, City of London, in 1854. He was Managing Director of the British Equitable from 1860 to death.

He took an active part in the affairs of the City, and was Chairman of the City Commission for Sewers in 1875. He was elected a Common Councillor for Vintry Ward in 1867, and served as Deputy of Vintry Ward from 1891 to death. He was also a Member of the City of London School Board.

Gover died at his residence, Casino House, Herne Hill, Dulwich, on 24 November 1894, aged 72 years.

NB: In 1922 the British Equitable merged with the State Assurance Company, which in 1922 became part of the Royal Exchange Group.

Grave 10227 Sq 116. Gothic chest tomb over brick vault. The vault was broken into and desecrated by vandals in the early 1980s, and restored in 2000. **Sources:** LCC; MI; British Census 1881; MEB Vol V 1912; Supple, Barry *The Royal Exchange Assurance - A History of British Insurance 1720-1970* 1970; *Trades directories*; Letter from Mr Thomson, archivist, Guardian Royal Exchange Assurance, dated 26 April 1982.

Revd HENRY WILLIAM GRESSWELL *MA* (1852-1924)
Priest and Religious Writer

Henry William Gresswell was born at Louth, Lincolnshire, in 1852, the eldest son of Daniel Gresswell, gentleman. He was educated at Lincoln College and Hertford College, Oxford, graduating BA in 1874, and proceeding MA in 1876. He was ordained deacon in 1875 and priest 1877. He was Curate of St Anne's Church, Hoxton, from 1876 to 1878, and held various curacies in London and elsewhere, before becoming Rector of Wendlebury, Bicester.

Mr Gresswell was the author of *Prayer and Temptation* (1900), and *Religion in Many Aspects* (1912). He died at the Rectory, Wendlebury, on 7 March 1924, aged 72 years.

Grave 35108 Sq 98. Tomb. **Sources:** LCC; MI; BC 1881; Alumni Oxon; Crockford.

JAMES GUDGE (1795-1857)
Clerk of Journals in the House of Commons

James Gudge of 6 St Germans Place, Blackheath, was Clerk of Journals to the House of Commons, Westminster, from 1835 to death. He tried to commit suicide by jumping into the River Thames on Wednesday 6 May 1857. He was pulled alive from the river, and died in Westminster Hospital on the following day.

Grave 947 Sq 81. Tomb. **Sources:** LCC; MI; MEB Vol I 1892; Rhind, Neil *Blackheath Village & Environs 1790-1970 V*ol II p 181.

WILLIAM JOHN HARRIS (1804-1894)
Landowner

William John Harris was born in Southwark about 1804. A wealthy land and property owner, he built, entirely at his own expense, Christ Church, Merton Lane, Mitcham. The church, a handsome building in the Gothic style, was erected in 1874 as a memorial to his beloved wife Mary Ann Harris who died in 1871. He also constructed a large family mausoleum at Nunhead.

He died at his residence, Gorringe Park House, Mitcham, Surrey, in December 1894, aged 90 years.

NB: The Harris mausoleum covered an area 22ft by 13ft and occupied a prominent position on the eastern side of the main avenue leading to the Anglican chapel. After being repainted and refurbished in 1939 it was completely destroyed by a German bomb on Thursday 17 October 1940.

Grave 11282 Sq 108. Mausoleum (grassed area, no trace of grave on site).
Sources: LCC; BC 1881; Thorne, James *Handbook to the Environs of London* Part II 1876 p 436; *Clergy List* 1889.

Commander **JOHN BLAKE HARROLD** *RNR, OBE, ISO, FCIS, FRCA, FZS* **(1876-1948)** *Former Registrar General of Shipping and Seamen*

John Blake Harrold was born at Salisbury, Wiltshire, in 1876, the eldest son of John Harrold, commercial traveller. He was educated at Wimborne Grammar School, Birkbeck College and King's College, London, and entered the Board of Trade in 1894. Commander Harrold was Registrar General of Shipping and Seamen from 1921 to 1938, and afterwards Honorary Pay Commander, Royal Naval Reserve. During World War II he served as Administrative Assistant to the 1st Somerset Battalion Home Guard. He died at 10 De Montfort Road, Streatham, on 8 October 1948, aged 72 years.
　　Grave 14154 Sq 141. Small cross. **Sources:** LCC; MI; BC 1881; KHB.

WILLIAM HARTREE *MICE* (1813-59)
Marine and Civil Engineer

William Hartree was born at Rotherhithe in December 1813, the son of William Hartree, gentleman. He was educated at the Merchant Taylors' School, Lewisham, and apprenticed to the marine engineer, John Penn FRS (1805-78), of Greenwich. He married Charlotte, the only sister of John Penn, and entered into partnership with his brother-in-law, taking an active part in the management of the firm.
　　He was devoted to literary pursuits and built a fine and well-stocked library at his residence at a cost of £10,000. He was also a keen astronomer and built an observatory in his garden which was within a mile of the Royal Observatory. He became ill while working on board HMS *Windsor Castle* at Devonport, and on returning to his residence at Morden Hill, Lewisham, suffered an attack of pleurisy. He died a few days later on 8 February 1859, aged 45 years.
　　Grave 5583 Sq 99. Solid granite tomb over vault by Gleaves of Greenwich. (The gun metal fittings surrounding the monument were reported stolen in the 1930s). **Sources:** LCC; MI: *Institution of Civil Engineers Minutes of Proceedings* Vol 19 pp 174-5; Letter from Richard Hartree 14 January 2002.

WILLIAM HENSHAW *Mus.D* (1791-1877)
Organist at Durham Cathedral

Dr Henshaw was organist at Durham Cathedral for almost half-a-century from 1813 to 1862, during which time be brought the cathedral choir up to a high standard of efficiency. He also composed chants. He died at 5 North Road, Clapham Park, on 30 September 1877, aged 86 years.
　　NB: Dr Henshaw's elder brother Thomas, organist at the Chapel Royal, St James's Palace, was accidentally burnt to death in 1868.
Grave 14457 Sq 61. Ledger tomb. **Sources:** LCC; MI; MEB Vol V 1912.

FRANCIS HILL (1801-1860)
Newspaper Editor

Francis Hill was for many years the City Editor of the 'Daily News' established at Bouverie Street in 1846. He died at his residence, Hope Town Lodge, Camberwell on 8 January 1860, aged 59 years.
   Grave 6038 Sq 64. Small monument in ruins. **Sources:** LCC; MI.

JENNY HILL stage name of Mrs JANE WOODLEY (1850-1896)
Music Hall Performer known as 'The Vital Spark'

Jane or Jenny Hill was born at Paddington in 1850, the only daughter of Michael Hill, a cabdriver. She made her stage debut aged seven at the Marylebone Theatre dressed as a goose, and first performed professionally at the age of ten for one shilling (5p) a night at Dr Johnson's Tavern, Bolt Court, Fleet Street.

At the age of twelve, young Jenny earned a living serving beer and singing and dancing in a public house in Bradford, and at the age of fourteen she appeared with George Leybourne at Manchester's London Music Hall.

She married John Wilson Woodley in 1867 (he died in 1890), an acrobat and pantomimist, who performed under the name of Jean Pasta. At the census in 1881, they were living at 9 Olney Street, Walworth, with their two daughters, Letitia Matilda, aged 13, and Jenny, aged 4. At some point after this date Woodley abandoned his wife and family.

Jenny Hill appeared at all the leading music halls billed as *The Vital Spark* and was a great success wherever she performed. She did male impersonations and sang and danced with immense vitality, and became famous for her cockney coster songs including 'The Coffee Shop Girl', 'Wot Cher 'Arry' and 'The boy I love is up in the gallery'. She also appeared at Tony Pastor's in New York. At the height of her fame, little Jenny was engaged by John Hollingshead for the Gaiety Theatre, London.

She kept the Albert Arms public house at Gladstone Street, Southwark, from 1882 to 1883, and afterwards bought the Gaiety Theatre, Southampton. The theatre opened on the 15 September 1884, and was burnt down two months later. In December 1893 she sold the contents of her house in Stockwell and went to live in South Africa. On falling ill she returned to England after just six months.

Little Jenny Hill was one of the Victorian Music Hall's brightest stars, and died at the home of her variety artiste daughter Letitia, alias Peggy Pryde, 241 Brixton Road, Stockwell, on Saturday 20 June 1896, aged 46 years. She was buried on Thursday 2 July 1896.

Grave 23061 Sq 143. Headstone with carved angel, and curbs (Mason: Daniel's Nunhead). **Sources:** LCC; MI; British Census 1881; MEB Vol V 1912; Hartnoll, Phyllis (ed) *The Oxford Companion to the Theatre* 1972; Busby, Roy *British Music Hall, an Illustrated Who's Who from 1850* 1976; Chance-Newton, H. *'Idols' of the Halls* 1975; Hudd, Roy *Music Hall* 1976; Honri, Peter *John Wilton's Music Hall - the handsomest room in town* 1985; Batten, Rex *Nunhead and the Music Hall* 2000.

RICHARD HOLLIER *FSA, FRGS* (1791-1852)
Antiquary and Traveller

Richard Hollier was a founder member of the Royal Geographical Society, his name appearing in the first list of Fellows published August 1830. In 1831 Hollier published *Glances at various objects during a nine week ramble through parts of France, Switzerland, Piedmont, Austrian Lombardy, Venice, Carinthis, the Tyrol, Schaffhausen, the bank of the Rhine, and Holland.*

In 1835 he was elected FSA, but little is known of his activities at the Society of Antiquaries, apart from the fact that in 1846 he exhibited a Roman steelyard weight from Nursling, Southampton. He died at his residence, Maze Hill, Greenwich on 26 January 1852, aged 61 years.

NB: Hollier amassed a large and valuable collection of books and paintings which his widow, Loetitia, bequeathed to Gresham College on her death in 1871.

Grave 2100 Sq 67. Box tomb over brick vault. **Sources:** LCC; MI; Letter from Mrs Christine Kelly, archivist, Royal Geographical Society 9th July 1981; Letter from Mr Thompson, General Secretary, the Society of Antiquaries, 8 January 1981.

TOM HOOD - *Thomas Hood the Younger* (1835-1874)
Editor, Novelist, Poet, and Artist

Thomas Hood the younger, better known as Tom Hood, was born at Lake House, Wanstead, Essex, on the 19 January 1835, the only son of the poet Thomas Hood. His family moved to Coblentz and later to Ostend after Tom's birth, and returned to England in 1840. He was educated at London, Lincoln, and Pembroke College, Oxford.

In 1858 he went to Cornwall where he was editor of the *Liskeard Gazette* for two years before becoming a clerk at the War Office. In 1865 he left the

Civil Service and became the editor of *Fun*, a popular satirical magazine and rival of *Punch*.

Tom inherited his father's talent for writing verse, and published his first poem 'Farewell to the Swallows' in 1853. His first book, *Pen and Pencil Sketches,* appeared in 1857. He was the author of several novels including *Captain Master's Children* (1865) which was perhaps his most successful. In 1867 he issued *Tom Hood's Comic Annual* which continued to be published after his death. In 1868 he wrote the preface to a collection of his father's work.

Favourite Poems, a collection of his own verse, was published posthumously.

He died at Gloucester Cottage, 92 Peckham Rye, on 20 November 1874, aged 39 years. He was laid to rest beside his wife Susan who had died a year earlier.

Grave 12168 Sq 59. Solid Granite Pedestal, *damaged. (Erected by a few friends and fellow workers.)* **Sources:** LCC; MI; DNB; MEB Vol I 1892; Browning, D. C. *Everyman's Dictionary of Literary Biography* 1958 p 329.

Revd Dr THOMAS HARTWELL HORNE *DD, FSA* (1780-1862)
Bible Critic and Bibliographer

Thomas Hartwell Horne was born in Chancery Lane, Holborn on 20 October 1780, the eldest son of William Horne, barristers' clerk. He was educated at Christ's Hospital, and became a barristers' clerk at the age of sixteen.

Horne studied and wrote in his spare time, often working through the night. His first publication, *A brief view of the necessity and truth of the Christian revelation*, was written when he was only eighteen. No less than 10 editions were published in England, and it was also published in the USA.

In 1806 he was Private Secretary to James Butterworth MP, and was Sub-Librarian at the Surrey Institute from 1809 to 1823. He was elected FSA in 1828. He published his *Introduction to the Critical Study and Knowledge of the Holy Scriptures* in 1818. This important work took him over seventeen years to complete and became the standard work on the subject. He received the degree of Doctor of Divinity from King's College, Aberdeen.

A former Wesleyan Methodist, in 1819 Mr Horne was ordained in the Church of England as Curate of Christchurch, Newgate Street. He joined the British Museum in 1824, and worked on the compilation of the British Museum Catalogue. He catalogued the Harleian manuscripts and edited Simeon's *Horae Homilecticae*, a 21 volume commentary on the Holy Bible. A prolific writer, he was the author of more than 50 works.

Dr Horne held various church offices and was Vicar of St Edmund the King and Martyr and St Nicholas Acons in the City of London, at the time of his death. He died at No 47 Bloomsbury Square on 27 January 1862.

Grave 5279 Sq 67. Tomb over brick vault. **Sources:** LCC; MI; DNB; MEB Vol I 1892; Proceedings of the Society of Antiquaries 1862; Browning, D. C. *Everyman's Dictionary of Literary Biography* 1958 pp 332-3; Thomas, Joseph *Lippincott's Universal Dictionary of Biography* 1915; *Alibone's Dictionary of Authors* 1877; *Chambers Encyclopaedia of English Literature* Vol II 1902.

GEORGE HOWELL *FSS* (1833-1910)
Trade Unionist, Labour Leader and former MP for Bethnal Green N E

George Howell was born at Wrington, near Bristol, on the 5 October 1833, son of Edwin John Howell, stonemason. He started work on a farm at the age of eight and was later apprenticed to a shoemaker who encouraged him in Christianity and politics.

In 1848 George Howell became a member of a Chartist group. He joined the Wesleyan Methodist Church and became a Sunday school teacher.

In 1855 he moved to London and found work in the building trade. He joined the London Order of the Operative Bricklayers' Society, and took an active part in trade union affairs. In 1865 he joined the Reform League 'to promote the conquest of political power by the working class'. He became the Secretary of the Reform League and organised demonstrations which succeeded in forcing Disraeli to accept an amendment to the Reform Bill of 1867. He was the first Secretary of the Trades Union Congress and Secretary to the Parliamentary Committee which promoted the Plimsoll Merchant Shipping Bill.

In 1880 George Howell lost his only son George Washington Taviner at the young age of 20. He was buried at Nunhead. The Howells were then living at 20 Camplin Street, Deptford.

As MP for Bethnal Green North East from 1885 to 1895, George Howell was one of the first working-class Members of Parliament. He was a Gladstone Liberal, opposed to the creation of a third (labour) party. Howell contributed to numerous publications and was the author of: *A Handy Book of the Labour Laws* 1876; *The Conflicts of Capital and Labour* 1878; *Trade Unionism, New and Old* 1891; *Labour Legislation, Labour Movements, and Labour Leaders* 1902. He died at Shepherd's Bush on 16 September 1910, aged 76 years.

Grave 15966 Sq 47. Headstone. *(Inscription barely legible).* **Sources:** LCC; MI; BC 1881; DNB; KHB 1908; Rogers, Frederick *Labour, Life and Literature* 1913 p 282; Leventhal, F. M. *Respectable Radical - George Howell and Working Class Politics* 1971; Bellamy, Joyce & Saville, John (eds) *Dictionary of Labour Biography* Vol II 1974; Finch, Harold *George Howell - Trade Unionist & Reformer* article in East London Record No 11, 1988 pp 2-9; Letter from Harold Finch dated 29 March 1982.

JAMES HOWELL (1787-1866)
Architect and Surveyor

James Howell was the nephew and pupil of William Pilkington (1758-1848). President of the Surveyors' Club in 1832 and 1849. he was for many years architect and district surveyor to the City of Westminster.

In 1841 he built Southwick House, Hampshire for Thomas Thislethwayte MP after the former house had been destroyed by fire.

Between 1856 and 1858 James Howell built houses in Vincent Square, Westminster, office buildings for the Equitable Gas Light Company at Pimlico, and stables in Regent Street (now Regency Street) Westminster.

He lived at No 1 Vincent Square and Reigate, Surrey, and died at Westminster on 31 July 1866, aged 79 years.

Grave 3137 Sq 77. Canopied tomb over brick vault, *probably designed by James Howell for the burial of his wife.* **Sources:** LCC; MI; 'The Builder' various years; Colvin, Howard *A Biographical Dictionary of British Architects 1600-1840* 1978; *Trades directories*.

FRANCIS JOSEPH HUMPHREYS *BA* (1862-1900)
Oxford Cox, University Boat Race 1884 and 1885

Francis Humphreys was born in 1862, the son of Edward Humphreys of Denmark Hill, solicitor. He was educated at Eton and Brasenose College, Oxford, and was coxswain of his college boat from 1882 to 1885. He coxed Oxford to victory in the 1885 University Boat Race.

Humphreys was admitted a solicitor in 1891, and was a partner in the firm of Grover, Humphreys and Son, at No 4 King's Bench Walk, Temple, from 1891 to death. He died at 2 Hyde Park Gate, London, on 29 March 1900, aged 38 years.

Grave 8849 Sq 127. Ledger tomb. **Sources:** LCC; MI; MEB Vol V 1912; Alumni Oxon.

*Lengthy inscription commemorating
Commander Charles Jones RN, KTS (1782-1847)*

BENJAMIN JOSEPH JACOB *JP* (1836-1918)
First Mayor of the Metropolitan Borough of Deptford

Benjamin Joseph Jacob was born at Deptford, the eldest son of Benjamin Jacob, lighterman and barge builder. He was educated at Colfe Grammar School, Lewisham, and was apprenticed to his father, eventually becoming the senior partner in the firm. He was twice Master of the Watermens' and Lightermens' Company, and a Past Master of the Worshipful Company of Carpenters. He was President of the Royal Asylum, Penge, and served on the old Vestry of Deptford; the Greenwich Board of Works; and the Greenwich Board of Guardians.

He was elected a Borough Councillor of the newly constituted Metropolitan Borough of Deptford in 1900, and became the first Mayor of Depford in 1901. He was again elected Mayor in 1902 for the coronation of Edward VII.

He was appointed JP for London in 1904, and Alderman of Deptford in 1909. He died at his residence, 29 Pepys Road, New Cross, Deptford, in January 1918, aged 81 years.

Grave 13637 Sq 147. Headstone, curbs and rails *(removed by Southwark Council for the laying out of a park picnic area in 1980).* **Sources:** LCC; BC 1881; KHB; Barnes, F. A. *Mayors of England and Wales* 1902.

JOSEPH JOHNSON (c1769-1869)
Centenarian

Joseph Johnson's address is recorded in the burial books as 'The Naval Reserve, Greenwich'. He died in May 1869, in his 101st year.

Grave 10438 Sq 83. Box tomb. Sources: LCC: MI (mostly illegible).

Commander CHARLES JONES *RN, KTS* (1782-1847)
Naval Hero

Charles Jones entered the Navy in November 1797, aged 15, as Midshipman on board HMS *Monmouth*. He served under Earl Vincent in the Channel fleet, and was wounded at the Battle of Copenhagen in 1801 on board HMS *Isis* under Lord Nelson. In 1803 Mr Jones served on board HMS *Vanguard* at the capture of *Le Duquesne* and *Le Creole* with the French General Morgan, and over 500 enemy troops on board. He was serving in same ship at the surrender of the town of St Marc, St Domingo.

In 1807 he joined Admiral Gambier's expedition to Copenhagen, when after a bombardment of three days the Danish fleet surrendered. In 1809 he commanded HMS *Indignant* in operations against Walcheren.

At the seaport of Flushing, Lieutenant Jones received the thanks of Sir Richard Strachan, and was presented by his fellow officers and ship's company with a sword for his gallantry in leading them into action. The inscription on his gravestone gives a brief description of his life and career and concludes with the statement, 'with other services in Europe, Africa and America, too numerous to particularise'. The rank of Retired Commander was conferred upon him in October 1837. He died at 69 Blackfriars Road, Southwark, on 19 January 1847, aged 65 years.

Grave 779 Sq 109. Headstone. **Sources:** LCC; MI; O'Byrne, W.R. *A Naval Biographical Dictionary* 1849.

CHARLES JONES *RCA, ARSA* (1836-1892)
Landscape and Animal Painter

Charles Jones was born in Mile End, East London, of Welsh parents. A watercolorist, he specialised in painting animals, especially cattle and sheep. He also painted landscapes. He exhibited over 100 paintings at the Royal Academy, the British Institution, New Water Colour Society, and other London galleries from 1860 to 1891. He was a Member of the Royal Cambrian Academy, and an Associate Member of the Royal Scottish Academy.

Jones died at his residence, Heathercroft, Balham Hill, Surrey, on 17 July 1892, aged 56 years. A posthumous exhibition of 200 paintings was held at Graves Gallery, Pall Mall, London, in April 1895.

NB: In 1983, Charles Jones's painting *An avenue with numerous sheep* was expected to fetch up to £3,000 at Christies.

Grave 21053 Sq 108. Headstone. **Sources:** LCC; MI; BC 1881; MEB Vol V 1912; Benezet, E. *Dictionnaire des Peintres, Sculpteurs, Dessinateurs et Graveurs* 1949; Nahum, Peter *Monograms of Victorian & Edwardian Artists* 1976 p 150.

WILLIAM JOYCE (c1816-1891)
Barrister and Legal Writer

William Joyce was born at St Pancras circa 1816, the second son of James Joyce of Chapel Street, Pentonville. He was a barrister of the Inner Temple in 1851 and Lincoln's Inn in 1860. He resided many years with his younger brother Samuel Joyce QC (1817-76) at 12 Endsleigh Street, Tavistock Square, St Pancras.

William Joyce was the author of *The Law and Practise of Injunctions in Equity and at Common Law* 2 vols (1872); *The Doctrines and Principles of the Law of Injunctions* (1877); and *Proposals for an Intellectual Franchise*.

He died at Thirlestane, Hampton Hill, Surrey, on 19 October 1891, aged 73 years.

Grave 13773 Sq 90. Monument and cross (damaged). **Sources:** LCC; MI; BC 1881; MEB Vol II 1897.

Grave of Joseph Lynn Leicester (1825-1903)
Labour Leader and Trade Unionist

JOSEPH LYNN LEICESTER (1825-1903)
Labour Leader and Trade Unionist: Former MP for South West Ham

Joseph Lynn Leicester was born in Warrington, Lancashire, on Christmas Eve 1825. From a poor working lad he became a master craftsman in the art of glass making, and took an active part in union affairs becoming the leader of the Flint Glass Workers Union. In 1867, as one of the London Working Men's Association leaders, he signed a 'Manifesto to the People of England on the Direct Representation of Labour in Parliament'.

As a leader of the Lib-Labs, Leicester was returned as the Member of Parliament for West Ham South in the General Election of 1885, but lost his seat to a Tory in the Gladstonian defeat of 1886. In 1892 he was again invited to contest West Ham South, but on finding the Independent Labour Party candidate Kier Hardy and a Tory standing against him, he withdrew from the contest, and Keir Hardy was returned as MP.

Leicester was a staunch advocate of temperance throughout his life, and took a leading part in the 'social elevation' of his fellow workmen. He died at 42 Malpas Road, Brockley, on 13 October 1903, aged 77 years. His gravestone bears the legend: *'Write him down as one that loved his fellow man'.*

Grave 27039 Sq 89. Headstone. Sources: LCC; MI; Cole, G. D. H. *British Working Class Politics 1832-1914* 1941; Bellamy, Joyce M. & Saville, John (eds) *Dictionary of Labour Biography* Vol III.

GEORGE LEWIS (c.1765-1867)
Centenarian

George Lewis died at Trundleys Lane, Deptford, in August 1867. His age is given as 102 in the burial records.

Grave 6988 Sq 12. *In 1914 the headstone was found to be in a dangerous condition and was laid down on the instructions of the Board of Directors.* **Sources:** LCC.

Captain JOHN LIDGETT (1800-1861)
Master Mariner and Shipowner

John Lidgett was born at Kingston-upon-Hull on the 18 December 1800, the fourth and youngest son of George Lidgett. His father, who was a pilot on the Humber, died when John was 8 years old. He attended the Trinity House School of Navigation in Hull through the generosity of a local merchant called Simpson, and went to sea as a cabin boy when he was 13. He became a Master Mariner at the age of 17 and Captain before reaching the age of 21.

Captain Lidgett was engaged in the Baltic trade, first sailing out of Hull, and later from London. He married in 1828, and became a ship-broker in

London in 1835. When shipping was depressed in 1841 Lidgett and his brother-in-law Joseph Shepherd, purchased Ichebod, a small uninhabited island off the coast of Namibia. Together they made a small fortune by shipping guano, which was used as agricultural fertiliser, from Ichebod to England. In 1847 Lidgett removed to Blackheath, and became an active member of the Greenwich Methodists, leading a class at Blackheath Chapel.

In 1855 Lidgett commissioned the building of a large mansion set in 35 acres of landscaped garden at Royal Tunbridge Wells, Kent. He named the house 'Kingston House' after his place of birth. The family moved into their new house in February 1857. Sadly, the move was marred that summer by the tragic death of his third son Samuel Lidgett (q.v.).

John Lidgett died at Blackheath, in the house of one of his sons, on the 17 June 1861, aged 60 years. Kingston House was sold to J. Remington Mills MP in 1867 who renamed it Kingswood House. John Lidgett's grandson was the well-known Methodist leader, the Revd Dr John Scott Lidgett CH, DD, LL.D (1854-1953).

Grave 1644 Sq 86. Chest tomb over brick vault. The vault was broken into and the contents desecrated in the mid-1980s. **Sources:** LCC; MI; Information from Miss McDougall; *Trades directories.*

SAMUEL JACOB LIDGETT BA (1833-1857)
Law Student

Samuel Lidgett was born in London on the 22 August 1833, the third son of John Lidgett (q.v.). He was educated at the City of London School and Trinity College, Cambridge, and was admitted a student at Lincoln's Inn in June 1857. Samuel was tragically killed on the 18 July 1857 when a cricket ball struck him on the chest whilst playing a friendly game of cricket on Tunbridge Wells Common.

Grave 1644 Sq 86. Lidgett family vault. **Sources:** LCC; MI; *Alumni Canta;* Letter from Miss E. McDougall; Contemporary newspaper cuttings.

Captain THOMAS LIGHT (1777-1863)
Charterhouse Brother or 'Codd'

According to William Kent (*Encyclopaedia of London* 1937), on the left of Preacher's Court and staircase 16 at the London Charterhouse, may be seen the following inscription: 'In this room lived Captain Thomas Light, whom Thackeray visited when writing the last chapters of the Newcombes'. Thackeray's Colonel Newcombe is based on Captain Light.

Captain Thomas Light, late of the 14th (Buckinghamshire) Regiment of Foot, was a pensioner (or Codd) at the London Charterhouse for fifteen years. The old soldier, who was blind, was cared for by his daughter. He died at the

London Charterhouse on 18 August 1863, aged 86 years.
Grave 7727 Sq 50. Headstone. **Sources:** LCC; MI; Kent, William *Encyclopaedia of London* 1937; Monsarratt, Ann *An Uneasy Victorian: Thackeray the Man* 1980 p 341.

Sir GEORGE THOMAS LIVESEY *MICE, MIME* (1834-1908)
Civil and Mechanical Engineer and Philanthropist

George Thomas Livesey was born at Islington on the 8 April 1834, the son of Thomas Livesey (q.v.). He was apprenticed to his father in 1848, and became Engineer and Manager of the South Metropolitan Gas Company in 1857. He succeeded his father as Secretary in 1871.

The Old Kent Road Gas Works were greatly enlarged under his management, and the South Metropolitan eventually became the largest supplier of gas in the South London area. He was appointed Chairman of the Company in 1885.

He was elected MICE in 1872 and served on the Council of the ICE from 1906 to death. He was also consulting engineer and advisor to several gas companies throughout the UK, including the Tynemouth, Coventry, and Aldershot companies.

A kind and generous man, Livesey gave large sums of money to many charities. He opened a working men's club in Peckham, and built Camberwell's first free public library, now the Livesey Museum, in the Old Kent Road. He also presented to the people of Deptford a large site at Telegraph Hill, Hatcham, which was opened as a public park in 1895. Always concerned for the welfare of his workers, he encouraged temperance and introduced a profit sharing scheme and paid holidays. He was on the War Office Committee for the employment of ex-servicemen, and was knighted in 1902. Sir George died at his residence, Shagbrook, Reigate, Surrey, on 4 October 1908. He was buried on 10 October 1908, the 37th anniversary of the death of his father. Over 7,000 gas workers lined the route of the funeral procession from the Old Kent Road Gas Works to Nunhead Cemetery.

Grave 29263 Sq 124. Red granite obelisk over brick grave. **Sources:** LCC; MI; BC 1881; DNB; Institution of Civil Engineers - Minutes of Proceedings (obituary) Vol 174; Blanch, W. H. *Ye Parish of Camberwell* 1875 p 347; KHB 1908; *Whitaker's Peerage* 1903; 'Segas Magazine' December 1982 pp 10 & 11.

THOMAS LIVESEY (1807-1871)
Gas Engineer

Thomas Livesey was originally employed by the Gas Light and Coke Company at Brick Lane in East London. In 1839 he became Manager of the South Metropolitan Gas Company, Old Kent Road, and was appointed Secretary and Manager of the company in 1842. He introduced many reforms in the status of his workers, including a sickness fund and a superannuation scheme. He was also a generous supporter of numerous local charities.

He resided at Peckham for many years before removing to Dulwich. He collapsed and died at the home of his physician on 10 October 1871.

***Grave 8132 Sq 65. Headstone.* Sources:** LCC; MI; MEB Vol II 1897; Blanch, W. H. *Ye Parish of Camberwell* 1875 p 347; 'Segas Magazine' December 1982.

WASHINGTON LYON (1819-1901)
Dyer and Bleacher

Washington Lyon was born at Clapton in 1819. He and his elder brother, John Andrew Lyon, removed to Camberwell when they were young men and established a large bleaching and dyeing works at St Mary-le-Strand House, the former Camberwell Parish Workhouse, in the Old Kent Road.

Washington Lyon was co-inventor, with his son Dr Thomas Glover Lyon MD *(see More Nunhead Notables)*, of a method of steam disinfection and sterilisation. He was for many years a Camberwell Vestryman, and died at his residence, 85 Asylum Road, Peckham, in May 1901, aged 82 years.

***Grave 14432 Sq 90. Pedestal surmounted by draped urn.* *(MI worn)*.
Sources: LCC; MI; BC 1881; Camberwell Vestry Annual Reports; Blanch, William H. *Ye Parish of Camberwell* 1875 pp 94, 184, 346.

WILLIAM LYON (1803-1874)
One of Queen Victoria's Gentlemen-at-Arms

William Lyon purchased his appointment as one of Queen Victoria's Gentleman-at-Arms in May 1844. He was present at the defence of St James's Palace during the Chartist riots of 1848 and resigned in 1852. He died at York House, Camberwell, in January 1874, aged 71 years.

***Grave 12692 Sq 50. Headstone.* Sources:** LCC; MI; Kearsley, Harvey *His Majesties Bodyguard of the Hon Corps of Gentleman-at-Arms* 1937.

HUGH SIMON MACLAUCHLAN (1852-1899)
Newspaper Editor

Hugh Simon Maclauchlan was born on the 15 December 1852, the son of the Revd Dr Thomas Maclauchlan of Moy, Scottish Presbyterian Divine and Gaelic Scholar. He was educated at Edinburgh Academy and Edinburgh University and became a journalist. He was editor of 'The Hampshire Telegraph and Portsmouth Evening News' from 1886 to 1892, and assistant editor of the 'London Star' from 1892.

Maclauchlan resided at 75 Croxted Road, West Dulwich. He died in Peckham House Lunatic Asylum, Peckham, on 28 December 1899, aged 47 years.

Grave 24991 Sq 144. Headstone. Sources: LCC; MI; WWW Vol 1.

GEORGE MANSELL (c1805-1870)
Newspaper Proprietor, Printer and Publisher

In the 1830s George Mansell was a printer and stationer at 3 King Street, Borough. He later removed his presses and printing works to numbers 67 & 68 Newcomen Street, Southwark, and in 1847 printed and published the 'South London News', the first local newspaper in South London.

He was long resident in the Parish of St Saviour's, Southwark, and served as Bell Warden of St Saviour's College Almshouses in West Dulwich. He died at his residence, Walnut Tree Lodge, Goose Green, East Dulwich, on 6 August 1870, aged 65 years.

Grave 11027 Sq 50. Headstone. Sources: LCC; MI; Blanch, W. H. *Ye Parish of Camberwell* 1875 p 365; Roberts, Sir Howard & Godfrey, Walter (eds) *Survey of London - Bankside* Vol XXII, 1950 p 33; Wilson, J. B. *The Story of Norwood* 1973 p 63.

GEORGE STEPHEN MANSELL (1841-1897)
Printer and Publisher

George Stephen Mansell was born in Southwark in 1841, the eldest son of George Mansell (q.v.). In 1868 he and his younger brother Thomas Colston Mansell (q.v.) founded the 'South London Observer and Camberwell and Peckham Times' at Church Street, Camberwell. The 'South London Observer' was a popular local newspaper and survived well into the 1960s when it was taken over by its competitor the 'South London Press'.

He died at his residence Walnut Tree Villa, Goose Green, East Dulwich, on 30 May 1897, aged 56 years.

Grave 11027 Sq 50. Headstone. Sources: LCC; MI; BC 1881; Blanch, William Harnett *Ye Parish of Camberwell* 1875 p 365.

THOMAS COLSTON MANSELL (1844-1895)
Newspaper Proprietor and Publisher

Thomas Colston Mansell was born in Southwark on the 16 August 1844, the son of George Mansell (q.v.). He was educated at Dulwich College and was joint founder with his elder brother George Stephen Mansell (q.v.), of the 'South London Observer and Camberwell and Peckham Times'. He also owned and published the 'South Metropolitan Journal'. He died at 189 Grove Lane, Camberwell, on 25 April 1895, aged 50 years.

Grave 22496 Sq 50. Headstone. **Sources:** LCC; MI; BC 1881; Blanch, W.H. *Ye Parish of Camberwell* 1875 p 365; Ormiston, Thomas Lane *Dulwich College Register 1619-1926* 1927 p 71.

HENRY WILLIAM GEGG MARKHEIM *MA* (1845-1906)
Former Government Inspector of Schools

Henry Markheim was born at Smyrna, Asia Minor, on the 26 January 1845, the second son of Harrison Alfred Markheim, missionary. He was educated at Lycee Charlemagne, Paris, and Queen's College, Oxford, and was elected a Fellow of Queen's College in 1871. He became a student of the Inner Temple in 1873. Markheim was HM Inspector of Schools, Committee of Council on Education, Whitehall, from 1876 to 1890. He died in St George's Hospital, Hyde Park Corner, London, on 22 November 1906, aged 61 years.

Grave 19510 Sq 114. Headstone (removed in 1980). **Sources:** LCC; MI; Alumni Oxon; Foster, J. *Oxford Men and their Colleges* 2 vols 1893.

PETER H. MARSH (1828-1909)
Crimean Veteran: One of the 'Noble Six Hundred'

Peter Marsh enlisted in the 17th Lancers in 1849 and rode in the famous *Charge of the Light Brigade* on the 25 October 1854. He was promoted to the rank of corporal in 1855, and transferred to the 8th (King's Royal Irish) Hussars in 1856.

Marsh became a member of the Balaclava Commemoration Society in 1879 and attended the first Balaclava Banquet in 1875. He atttended his last Annual Dinner in 1908, and died at his residence, 312 Southwark Park Road, Bermondsey, on 5 February 1909, aged 81 years.

Grave 28742 Sq 138. Granite ledger tomb. **Sources:** LCC; MI; Lummis, W. M. and K. G. Wynn *Honour the Light Brigade* 1977 p 285.

Revd WILLIAM GEORGE MARTIN MA (1822-1892)
Founder of the Licenced Victuallers' Choral Association

William George Martin was born in Exeter, Devon, on the 18 February 1822, the son of George Martin, cabinet maker. He was educated at St John's College, Cambridge, and took holy orders in 1848. In 1850, after a short curacy at St Mary Magdalene, Southwark, he was appointed Chaplain of the Licenced Victuallers' Association Chapel, Asylum Road, Peckham.

An accomplished musician, Mr Martin founded the Licenced Victuallers' Choral Association, and assisted in the choral services at the wedding of the Prince of Wales (later King Edward VII) at St George's Chapel, Windsor. In 1871, on completion of 21 years service as Chaplain of the Licenced Victuallers' Association, he was presented with 1,000 guineas (£1,050) at a banquet held in his honour at the Crystal Palace.

He was Chaplain of the LVA for 42 years, and died at the Parsonage, Asylum Road, Peckham, on 9 April 1892, aged 70 years. NB: He was laid to rest in the Beardmore family vault at Nunhead, alongside his father-in-law Joseph Beardmore, marine engineer, and his brother-in-law William Beardmore (q.v.).

Grave 12600 Sq 124. Large monument over vault. **Sources:** LCC; MI; BC 1881; MEB Vol VI 1921; Blanch, W. H. *Ye Parish of Camberwell* 1875 p 213; *Clergy List* 1889.

Commander EDWARD MAXEY RN (1790-1871)
Royal Naval Officer

Edward Maxey was born on the 5 February 1790, the second son of the Revd Lewis Maxey, Rector of Byford, Hereford. He entered the Navy in 1804 as First Class Volunteer on board HMS *Utrecht,* and joined HMS *Intrepid* in 1805.

Mr Maxey took part at the capture of Capri in 1806, and was present at the siege of Gaeta. As Masters Mate on board HMS *Norge* he assisted at the embarkation of troops after the Battle of Corunna, and co-operated at the defence of Cadiz. In 1811 he sailed to the arctic in pursuit of the American frigate *President.*

In 1814 Mr Maxey was promoted to the rank of Lieutenant whilst serving with the Duke of Clarence in the yacht *Royal Charlotte.* He served on the American, Home and West India Stations. In 1829 Lieutenant Maxey married Eliza, a daughter of Joseph Edye, Alderman of Bristol. He was promoted to the rank of Commander, and died at 75 New Church Road, Camberwell, on 24 November 1871, aged 81 years.

Grave 11632 Sq 65. Pedestal. **Sources:** LCC; MI; O'Byrne, W. R. *A Naval Biographical Dictionary* 1849.

HENRY EDWARD MAYO (1847-1891)
Surrey Cricketer

Henry Mayo was born at South Lambeth on the 13 November 1847, the son of John Ryall Mayo, solicitor of Kennington and Peckham Rye. He was a middle order right-hand batsman and right-hand fast round-arm bowler. Described as a very fair all-round amateur cricketer, he played 14 matches for Surrey County Cricket Club during the seasons 1868, 1869 and 1870.

Mayo, who was by profession a solicitor's clerk, died at 46 Cranmer Road, North Brixton, on 30 October 1891, aged 44 years.

Grave 11979 Sq 49. Headstone (not located). **Sources:** LCC; BC 1881; *Who's Who of Cricketers* 1984; Green, Benny (ed) *The Wisden Book of Cricketers' Lives* 1986 p 608.

WILLIAM McCORMICK (1801-1878)
MP for Londonderry 1860-65

William McCormick of Lisahawley House, County Londonderry, was born in Ireland and was living in Liverpool by 1834. A contractor for public works at 41 Parliament Street, Westminster, he served as Member of Parliament for Londonderry from 1860 to 1865. McCormick was also a magistrate for Londonderry. He died at 17 Augers Terrace, Regent's Park, London, on 12 June 1878, aged 77 years.

NB: His son, the Revd Dr Joseph McCormick (1834-1914), was Rector of Piccadilly, and his grandson, the Rev William Patrick Glynn McCormick DSO (1877-1940), was Chaplain to HM King George VI.

Grave 10822 Sq 136. Small cross. **Sources:** LCC; MI; MEB Vol II 1897.

ALFRED MELLOR *JP* (1842-1931)
Army Officer & Magistrate

Alfred Mellor was born in London on the 18 May 1842, the fourth son of the Rt Hon Sir John Mellor PC, of Kingsdowne House, Dover, and Elizabeth Cooke Moseley, only daughter of William Moseley, of Peckham Rye. He served as a Lieutenant in the 8th (King's) Regiment of Foot, and as JP for Devon and Somerset. He resided at Otterhead, Honiton, Devon, and died at his London residence, 42 St John's Wood Court, St Marylebone, on 18 March 1931, aged 88 years.

NB: A younger brother, Edward Daniel Mellor (q.v.), was Chief Clerk in Chancery, Royal Courts of Justice, and his elder brother, the Rt Hon John Mellor PC, was Deputy Speaker of the House of Commons 1893-5.

Grave 15789 Sq 68. Small cross. **Sources:** LCC; MI; BC 1881; *Burke's Family Records* 1897 pp 429-430; KHB 1926.

EDWARD DANIEL MELLOR *MA* (1843-1890)
Chief Clerk in Chancery, Royal Courts of Justice

Edward Daniel Mellor was born in London on the 28 July 1843, the fifth son of the Rt Hon Sir John Mellor PC, of Kingsdowne House, Dover, and Otterhead, Devon. He was a younger brother of Alfred Mellor (q.v.).

Edward Mellor was educated at Trinity Hall, Cambridge, and admitted a solicitor in 1869. He was Chief Clerk in Chancery at the Royal Courts of Justice at the time of his death. He died unmarried at 27 Albion Street, Paddington, on 8 November 1890, aged 47 years.

Grave 20119 Sq 68. Tomb. **Sources:** LCC; MI; BC 1881; Alumni Canta; *Burke's Family Records* 1897 pp 429-30.

CHARLES HENRY MILLS (1867-1948)
Professional Cricketer

Charles Henry Mills was the second son of Charles and Sarah Mills. His father, was an artist engraver from Leeds, and his mother came from Co Durham. In 1866 the family removed to Peckham, Surrey, where on the 26 November 1867 Charles Henry Mills was born. In 1881 the family's address was 77 East Surrey Grove, Peckham.

A right-hand batsman, and right-arm medium pace bowler, Charles Henry Mills played in just two matches for Surrey County in 1888. In 1889 he left England for South Africa, where he became a coach for the Cape Town Cricket Club. He also played cricket for Kimberley in 1889 and 1890, and for the Western Province from 1892 to 1895. He played in just one test match for South Africa during the 1891/2 season.

Little is known about Charles Mills after 1895; he most probably returned to the UK at the beginning of the 20th century. He died at No 21 Herron Street, Southwark, on 26 July 1948, aged 80 years.

Grave 42184 Sq 45. Common grave. **Sources:** LCC; BC 1881; Bailey, Thorn, Wynne-Thomas *Who's Who of Cricketers* 1984.

Captain WILLIAM MITCHELL (1777-1848)
Waterloo Veteran

William Mitchell was born on the 27 January 1777. As Paymaster to the Royal Regiment of Foot, this officer saw 'much rough service' having accompanied his regiment to Montevideo, Sicily, and Flanders. He served throughout the Peninsular Campaign and was present at the Battle of Waterloo in 1815.

Captain Mitchell died at No 9 Grosvenor Road, Camberwell, on 11 April 1848, aged 71 years.

Grave 1115 Sq 81. Headstone. **Sources:** LCC; MI.

WILLIAM RICHARD MORRIS *MICE* (1808-1874)
Civil Engineer

William Richard Morris was born on the 24 October 1808, the only son of Joshua Morris of Greenwich. He was articled to Charles Alexander Weir, Manager of the Kent Water Works, under whose instructions he built roads in the Grand Duchy of Mecklenburg Schwerin and assisted in the erection of Hammersmith Suspension Bridge. He also superintended the completion of Southend Pier under Sir William Heygate which in 1845 was the longest pleasure pier in England.

Morris assisted in the design and erection of the gas works at Vauxhall, Lewes, and Stratford-upon-Avon, and was engaged by the Grand Surrey Canal Dock Company. He was for 38 years Engineer and Manager to the Kent Water Works, and the first engineer to use the double-acting pump in combination with the single acting Cornish engine for waterworks, therefore avoiding the need of a standpipe. In 1834 he published *A Survey of the Parish of Greenwich*. He was elected MICE in 1856. He died of apoplexy at the Kent Water Works, Mill Lane, Deptford, on 11 January 1874, aged 65 years.

Grave 1256 Sq 125. Pedestal (ruins). **Sources:** LCC; MI; MEB Vol VI 1921; *Institution of Civil Engineers 'Memoirs'* Vol 35 1875.

EGBERT MOXHAM *AMICE* (1822-1864)
Architect and Civil Engineer

Egbert Moxham was born on the 3 February 1822. He studied architecture in the office of Thomas Brown of Edinburgh, and later practised on his own account as an architect and surveyor at Neath, West Glamorgan. He designed a church at Skewen, plus an abattoir, a chapel, a school-house, and several mansions at Neath. Moxham later turned his attention to railways and carried out surveys for the Welsh, Midland, and Southampton Junction Railways. He was admitted AMICE 1851, and died at Maze Hill, Greenwich, on 4 September 1864, age 42 years.

Grave 8238 Sq 83. Headstone. **Sources:** LCC; MI; Information supplied by the Institution of Civil Engineers 1981.

HARRY MUNRO (1830-1876)

Harry Munro was the second son of Sir Charles Munro, 9th baronet of Foulis who died in 1886, and the father of Sir George Hamilton Munro, 12th baronet, and Sir Arthur Talbot Munro, 13th baronet. He died at No 2A Selden Road, Nunhead, on 26 September 1876, aged 46 years.

Grave 13789 Sq 120. Headstone (with family crest). **Sources:** LCC; MI; Fox-Davies, A. C. *Armorial Families* 1927.

GASTON MURRAY (1826-1889)
Actor

Gaston Murray whose real name was Garstin Parker Wilson, was born in Pimlico, Middlesex, in 1826. He first appeared on stage in *The Happiest Day of My Life* at the Prince's Theatre, Glasgow, in June 1854. His first London appearance was at the Lyceum in March 1855 when he played Tom Saville in *Used Up*. Between 1854 and 1871 he appeared in over twenty different plays at the Adelphi, the Olympic, St James's, and the Haymarket theatres. His last appearance was as Mr Pickwick at the Standard Theatre in 1872.

In 1872 he was treasurer to the Earl of Londesborough, and produced *Babil and Bijou at Covent Garden*. He was Secretary of the General Theatrical Fund 1880 to 1882. He died at 19 Loughborough Road, Brixton, on 8 August 1889, aged 63 years. NB: His wife was the actress Mary Frances Wilson (q.v.), and his elder brother Henry Leigh Murray (1820-70) was a well-known actor.

Grave 9718 Sq 27. Ledger. **Sources:** LCC; MI; BC 1881; DNB: MEB Vol II 1897.

ANTHONY KING NEWMAN (c1774-1858)
Printer and Publisher of Children's Books

Anthony King Newman was a London bookseller and joined the publisher William Lane as his partner from 1802 to 1808. He later took over and ran the Minerva Press at 32-33 Leadenhall Street for 28 years from 1820 to 1848. Newman also had an arrangement with the book publisher Dean and sold Dean's children's books under his own imprint. He died at 17 Clarence Street, Greenwich, on 11 August 1858, aged 84 years.

Grave 5314 Sq 143. Obelisk *(with coat of arms).* **Sources:** LCC; MI; Muir, P. *Victorian Illustrated Books* 1971; *Trades directories.*

ARTHUR HARRISON NEWMAN *FRIBA, FSI* (1855-1922)
Architect and Surveyor

Arthur Harrison Newman was born in Camberwell on the 19 May 1855, the son of Arthur Shean Newman (q.v.), architect. His grandfather was John Newman FSA. He was articled to his father at the age of 16, eventually taking over the practice at Tooley Street, Southwark. He designed several churches between 1878 and 1890 including: St Augustine's, Stepney; St Paul's, Old Ford; and St George's, Westcombe Park, Blackheath. He also carried out restoration work to Kingsbury Church. He was elected FSI in 1880 and FRIBA in 1891. He died 17 October 1922.

Grave 12230 Sq 50. Headstone. **Sources:** LCC; MI; BC 1881; DNB; Fellowship Nomination Paper and information supplied by RIBA May 1982.

ARTHUR SHEAN NEWMAN FRIBA (1828-1873)
Architect and Surveyor

Arthur Shean Newman was born at the Old Bridge House, Southwark, in 1828, the son of the noted architect and antiquary John Newman FSA (1786-1859). In partnership with Arthur Billing, he designed many churches throughout the country including Holy Trinity, Penge, 1872. He was for many years Surveyor to Guy's Hospital and the Parish of St Olave, Southwark. He lived many years at Peckham, and died at 22 Belmont Hill, Lee, Kent, on 3 March 1873.
  Grave 12230 Sq 50. Headstone (with carved armorial bearings). **Sources:** LCC; MI; DNB; MEB Vol II 1897.

EDWARD NEWMAN FLS, FZS, FRMS, M. Imp. LCA (1801-1876)
Botanist, Entomologist and Ornithologist

Edward Newman was born at Hampstead on the 13 May 1801, the eldest of four sons of George and Ann Newman. His parents were members of the Society of Friends. In 1812 he was sent to a boarding school at Painswick, Gloucestershire, leaving at the age of 16 to join his father's business as a woolstapler at Godalming. He used to spend his spare time exploring the beautiful Surrey countryside.

In 1826 he obtained a rope-walk at Deptford, and transformed a large garden adjoining the rope-walk into a nature area especially to enable him to study the habits of insects.

He wrote numerous natural history articles which were published in 'Chambers Journal' and other magazines under the pen-name 'Rusticus'. He wrote under several pseudonyms including 'Corderius Secundus' and 'END' as well as his own name. An original member of the Entomological Society, he was elected FLS in 1833 and FZS in 1839. In 1840 he sold his business and joined the printer George Luxford as a partner in the publishing house at Ratcliffe Highway.

Newman was the founder and editor of the 'Entomologist', 'Zoologist' and 'Phytologist'. From 1858 he was Editor of 'The Field'. He wrote and published many papers and books on all kinds of natural history subjects. His best known works include: *A Grammar of Entomology* (1835*), A History of British Ferns* (1840), *A Familiar Introduction to the History of Insects* (1841*), The Insect Hunters* or *Entomology in Verse* (1857), *British Moths: Nocturni* (1862*), Bird-Nesting: the*

Nest and Eggs of Every British Bird (1862), *A Dictionary of British Birds* (1866*), Illustrated Natural History of British Moths* (1869), and *Illustrated Natural History of British Butterflies* (1871).

Newman was a member of the Imperial Academy of Leopold Charles of Austria and 'one of the forty most distinguished naturalists in the world'. He died at his residence, 7 York Grove, Peckham, on 12 June 1876, aged 75 years. He was interred in the Dissenters' ground at Nunhead.

Grave 2740 Sq 128. Headstone. Sources: LCC; MI; DNB; MEB Vol II 1897; Kirk, J. F. *Dictionary of Authors Supplement* 1891; 'The Leisure Hour' No 1500, 25 Sept 1880 pp 629-631; Newman, Thomas Prichard *Memoir of the Life and Works of Edward Newman* 1876.

JOHN NICOL *MD* (1798-1874)
Physician and Surgeon

Dr John Nicol was Physician to St John's Hospital, La Paz, Peru, and a former President of the La Paz Medical Tribunal. He died at 113 Douglas Street, Deptford, on 10 November 1874, aged 76 years.

Grave 5412 Sq 79. Headstone. Sources: LCC; MI.

JOHN SPENCER NOLDWRITT *FRAS, FRGS* (1815-1891)
Lecturer

John Spencer Noldwritt was born at Clerkenwell the son of John Noldwritt. He was Secretary of the Walworth Literary Institution for more than 40 years, and gave much time and money to the cause. In 1862, he built at his own expense, a new reading room at Carter Street, Walworth. He was a popular lecturer on many subjects including, astronomy, natural history and ethnology. He was elected FRGS in 1876. Noldwritt died at his residence, 44 Benhill Road, Camberwell, on 1 January 1891, aged 75 years.

Grave 3179 Sq 123. Headstone. Sources: LCC; MI; BC 1881; MEB Vol II 1897; Blanch, W. H. *Ye Parish of Camberwell* 1875 pp 358-9; Letter from Mrs Kelly, archivist, Royal Geographical Society 31 March 1983.

Admiral MATTHEW STAINTON NOLLOTH *RN, FRGS, FMS* (1810-82)

Matthew Stainton Nolloth was born in 1810, the fifth son of John Nolloth, Assistant Secretary of the Navy Board. He entered the Navy in 1824 at the age of 14, and obtained his first commission at the age of 28. In 1843, as Senior Lieutenant on board HMS *Childers*, he distinguished himself in operations in the Yang-Tse-Kiang, China.

He was promoted to the rank of Commander in 1846, and given command of HMS *Frolic* on station at Cape Town. In 1856 he carried the great explorer

Dr David Livingstone from Quilimane to Mauritius.

As Commander Nolloth he surveyed the west coast of South Africa, and gave his name to Port Nolloth. He was promoted to the rank of Captain in 1856. On returning to England in 1857 he published *Notes during a Cruise in the Mozambique* and was elected FRGS. He was also the author of *On the Submergence of the Atlantic Telegraph Cable* published in 1858.

He was a Member of the Society of Arts and a Fellow of the Marine Society, and served on the Committee for the Protection of Ships from Fire and from Loss by Sinking. He retired in 1870, and was given the rank of Rear Admiral Retired in 1874 and Vice-Admiral Retired in 1879. He died at 13 North Terrace, Peckham Road, Camberwell, on 11 May 1882, aged 72 years.

Grave 13733 Sq 68. Large canted ledger over vault. Sources: LCC; MI; MEB Vol II 1897; Haydn, Joseph *Haydn's Book of Dignities* 3rd Edition 1894 p 850; O'Byrne, W. R. *A Naval Biographical Dictionary* 1849; Information about Port Nolloth supplied by the South African Embassy 1981; Letter from Mrs Kelly, archivist, Royal Geographical Society 1982.

CICELY NOTT (1832-1900)
Actress and Singer

Cicely Nott was the stage name of Mrs Sarah Ann Adams. She was born at Gosport, Hampshire, in 1832, the daughter of Elijah Luke Hatch Harris.

A prima donna at Jullien's promenade concerts at Drury Lane Theatre in 1852, she first performed as an actress in 1854 at the Theatre Royal, Plymouth. She played Shakespearean parts in Ireland, Brighton and Manchester, and played Little Boy Blue in *Little Red Riding Hood* at the Lyceum, London, on Boxing Day 1861. She sang the principal soprano part in *Manfred* at Drury Lane on the 10 October 1863, and played Pollio in *The Pretty Druidess* at the opening night of the Charing Cross Theatre on the 19 June 1869. One of her last performances was as Clarissa in *Give a Dog a Bad Name* at the Adelphi Theatre in 1876.

Cicely Nott was twice married. Her first husband Pio Bellini (q.v.) died in 1858. She married secondly, in 1860, Samuel Adams the proprietor of several London and provincial theatres. She bore Adams a son and four daughters, one of whom, Ada Blanche (q.v.), was principal boy at Drury Lane. She retired on annuity from the Royal General Theatrical Fund, and died at 23 Albert Square, Clapham Road, South Lambeth, on 3 January 1900, aged 67 years. She was buried at Nunhead in the same grave as her parents and first husband.

NB: Sam Adams predeceased her in 1893, and lies buried at Norwood Cemetery.

Grave 25248 Sq 125. Headstone. Sources: LCC; MI; BC 1881; MEB Vol VI 1921; Chance-Newton, H. *Idols of the Halls - being my Music Hall Memories* 1928.

GEORGE COLWELL OKE (1821-1874)
Chief Clerk to the Lord Mayor of London and Legal Writer

George Colwell Oke was born at St Columb Major, Cornwall, on 8 February 1821, the son of William Oke. He commenced work as an accountant in a solicitors office, and was Assistant Clerk to the Newmarket Bench of Justices in 1848. In 1855 he became Assistant Clerk at the Mansion House, and was Chief Clerk to the Lord Mayor of London from 1864 to death.

Oke published many standard legal works. His first *The Synopsis of Summary Convictions* was published in 1848. This was followed by *The Magisterial Synopsis* in 1849, the 14th edition of which was published in 1893. His last work *The Laws as to Licencing Inns* was published in 1872. He died at his residence, Rosedale, St Mary's Road, Peckham, on 9 January 1874, aged 52 years.

Grave 12654 Sq 68. Cross over vault. **Sources:** LCC; MI; DNB; MEB Vol II 1897; *Alibone's Dictionary of Authors* 1877.

RICHARD PENNINGTON *JP* (1833-1910)
President of the Incorporated Law Society 1892

Richard Pennington was born at Kendal, Westmorland, in 1833, the fourth son of James Pennington, a leading authority on currency. A solicitor at Lincolns Inn, he was Chairman of the Legal and General Life Assurance Company, Chairman of the Law Accident Society, and Chairman of the Solicitors' Law Stationery Society. He was also a director of several organisations including the Solicitors' Benevolent and Governesses' Benevolent Institutions, and President of the Incorporated Law Society 1892 to 1893.

Pennington lived at Latrigg, Windermere, and was a JP for Westmorland. He died at his London residence, Birchwood, Sydenham Hill, Camberwell, on 13 July 1910.

Grave 10330 Sq 71. Kerbstones. **Sources:** LCC; MI; BC 1881; KHB 1895 and 1908.

SARAH CROSS POOLE (1799-1861)
Actress and Singer

Sarah Cross Poole was the daughter of John Poole of the Parish of Christ Church, Southwark. She was for many years a member of the Drury Lane Theatre Company, and died at 198 Blackfriars Road, Southwark, on 2 July 1861, aged 62 years. NB: She bequeathed £1,000 to London charities.

Grave 187 Sq 155. Headstone. Her gravestone bears the following legend: *This grave is closed forever, to be repaired in perpetuity by the Company, she being the last of the family.* **Sources:** LCC; MI.

Revd CHARLES PREST (1806-1875)
Wesleyan Minister and Religious Writer

Charles Prest was born at Bath, Somerset, on the 16 October 1806, and became a Wesleyan Methodist Minister in 1829. His first ministry was at Bristol from 1830 to 1833, after which he ministered at Manchester before returning to Bristol in 1836. He also ministered at Birmingham, Hull and London, including a short spell at Wesley's Chapel in the City Road.

A staunch protestant, Prest was serious, direct and practical. He was Secretary to the Committee of Privileges from 1857 to death, and pioneered, with Dr Luke Wiseman, Methodism's 'Home Missions Movement'. He actively promoted the building of chapels and supported the army and the navy.

He was the author of *The Home Work of the Wesleyan Methodists* (1855), *Fourteen Letters on the Home Work of Wesleyan Methodists* (1856), and *The Witness of the Holy Spirit* (1864).

In 1862 he was President of the Methodist Conference at Camborne, Cornwall. He died at his residence in Burnt Ash Lane, Lee, Kent, on 25 August 1875, aged 68 years. NB: A mural tablet to his memory was erected in Wesley's Chapel, City Road, London.

Grave 13495 Sq 149. Tomb. Sources: LCC; MI; MEB Vol II 1897; Davey, Cyril J. *The Methodist Story* 1955 pp 136-138, 150; Information from Gordon Johnson 1985.

SYDNEY PRESTIGE *AMICE* (1856-1933)
Civil Engineer

Sydney Prestige was born at Deptford on the 26 September 1856, the son of John Theodore Prestige of Hulme House, Brockley. He was a pupil of J & G Rennie from 1872 to 1877, and became Outdoor Manager to Josiah Stone & Company of Deptford in 1877. He was responsible for fitting pumping systems to several ships, including the iron-clad HM *Independencia,* and *Foo-Shoo* of the Imperial Japanese Navy.

In 1878 he was appointed Works Manager at Stone's. He designed and constructed appliances for several water companies in England, India and Brazil. He also designed and supervised the building of Stone's general engineering works at Arklow Road, Deptford, which covered three acres of former market gardens and opened in 1881.

Sydney Prestige became a director of Josiah Stone & Co, and died at his residence 'Bernersmede' Blackheath Park, on 19 October 1933, aged 77 years.

Grave 20843 Sq 139. Vault. Sources: LCC; MI; BC 1881; Letter from Mr W. A. Morris, archivist, Institution of Civil Engineers 4th May 1982; Rhind, Neil *Blackheath Village & Environs* Vol II 1983 pp 97 & 101; Gurnett, Peter *Stone's of Deptford* Lewisham Local History Society 's Transactions 1986/7.

BURTON EDWARD RAVENSCROFT (1812-1873)
Wigmaker and Law Printer

Burton Edward Ravenscroft was born on the 8 December 1812, the eldest son of Humphrey William Ravenscroft (q.v.), and Julianna Burton. He was in business with his father at No 3 Serle Street, Lincoln's Inn Fields, and later as a law printer at No 18 Took's Court, Chancery Lane. When his father retired in 1844, he joined his brothers in running the family wig business. He died 27 January 1873, aged 61 years.
   Graves 4654, 12344 and 12345, Sq 89. Obelisk over brick graves (collapsed) by Daniel & Wilks. **Sources:** LCC; MI; Ravenscroft W & R B, *The Family of Ravenscroft* 1915; Todd, William B. *Directory of Printers and Others in Allied Trades* 1972.

BURTON CLEMENT RAVENSCROFT (1844-1921)
Wig and Robe Maker

Burton Clement Ravenscroft was born in London, the eldest son of Burton Edward Ravenscroft (q.v.), and grandson of Humphrey William Ravenscroft (q.v.). Although a qualified architect and surveyor, he later took over the running of the family wig business at Lincoln's Inn. In 1902 the wig business merged with Ede & Son, the famous robe making concern, to form Ede, Son and Ravenscroft. Rosa Ede, the proprietor of Ede & Son, was Burton Clement Ravenscroft's sister.
   He died at 56 Elmbourne Road, Balham, in March 1921, aged 76 years. NB: The firm of Ede & Ravenscroft, which still exists at Chancery Lane, was run by members of the Ravenscroft family until the 1970s.
   Grave 15068 Sq 89. Pedestal. **Sources:** LCC; MI; British Census 1881; Ravenscroft W. & R. B. *The Family of Ravenscroft* 1915; Campbell, Una *Robes of the Realm* 1989 p 26; *Trades directories*.

FRANCIS WALL MACKENZIE RAVENSCROFT (1828-1902)
Entrepreneur

Francis Ravenscroft was born in Westminster, the seventh son of Humphrey William Ravenscroft (q.v.). At the age of 20 he became a student at the Mechanics Institute and was elected to its management committee. In 1851 he founded the Birkbeck Bank and Building Society, and acquired the former buildings of Birkbeck College for his new bank. He personally guaranteed the cost of a brand new college building to replace the old one, and collected £4,000 towards its erection.
   Francis Ravenscroft was a generous benefactor of Birkbeck College and Governor for more than fifty years. He was elected a Member of the Society of

Arts in 1871.

In 1893 Ravenscroft built Queen's Hall, the original home of Henry Wood's Promenade Concerts, at Langham Place, Regent Street. In 1896 he built a bank in Chancery Lane to the designs of T. E. Knightley. The exterior of the new nine-storey Birkbeck Bank was decorated with bright green, and biscuit and brown Carraraware, by Royal Doulton, and the interior of the domed banking hall contained scenes illustrating various trades, industries, commerce and banking.

Francis Ravenscroft died suddenly at his residence, 'Birkbeck Lodge' 64 Springfield Road, St John's Wood, on 15 June 1902, aged 73 years.

NB: After his death the bank was managed by his third son Clarence. In 1911 the Birkbeck Bank closed its doors for the last time. Some of its assets and the imposing building in Chancery Lane were taken over by Westminster Bank. Regrettably, the handsome bank building was demolished in 1965. Queen's Hall had been destroyed by enemy action in 1941.

Grave 9662 Sq 88. Large octagonal monument surmounted by cross.
Sources: LCC; MI; BC 1881; 'Journal of the Society of Arts' June 20 1902; Ravenscroft W. & R. B. *The Family of Ravenscroft* 1915; Burns, Delisle *Birkbeck College 1823-1923* 1924; Gregory, T. E. *Westminster Bank Thro' a Century* 1936; Atterbury, P, and Irvine, Louise *The Doulton Story* 1979 pp 78-79.

HUMPHREY WILLIAM RAVENSCROFT (1784-1851)
Peruke Maker - Inventor of the Patent Forensic Wig

Humphrey William Ravenscroft was born at No 3 Serle Street, Lincoln's Inn Felds on the 4 December 1784, the eldest son of Thomas Ravenscroft, peruke maker of Market Drayton and London. The Ravenscroft family originated in Cheshire but several had settled in London by the close of the 17th century.

The wig making business was founded by Humphrey's grandfather also Thomas, at Serle Street in 1726. Humphrey took over the business following his father's death in 1806. He patented his famous forensic wig in 1822, and was the first wig maker to use white horse hair superseding the use of hair powder. Humphrey Ravenscroft's patent wig is an essential part of a barrister's attire, and continues to be manufactured by Ede & Ravenscroft of Chancery Lane to this day.

After retiring from the family wig making business in 1844, he ran an academy for young ladies at Coburg Road, Camberwell, and died at Camberwell, on 29 June 1851, aged 66 years.

Grave 1978 Sq 89. Headstone. **Sources:** LCC; MI; MEB Vol III 1901; Ravenscroft W. & R. B. *The Family of Ravenscroft* 1915; Campbell, Una *Robes of the Realm* 1989 p 27-30.

EDWARD COCKBURN RAVENSHAW *FRGS* (1804-1877)
Bengal Civil Servant

Edward Cockburn Ravenshaw was the son of John Goldsboro' Ravenshaw, Chairman of the Hon. East India Company, and a brother of the Revd Thomas Ravenshaw (q.v.). He went to India at the age of 18, and was appointed Second Assistant to the Secretary to the Government in the Secret and Political Department, becoming First Assistant in 1824. In 1828 he was Officiating Deputy Secretary to the Government in the Territorial Department.

He was appointed Additional Judge of Patna, and Sessions Judge for the trial of all commitments of thugs by Captain Ramsay at Chuprah in 1837, and was Commissioner of Revenue at Patna in 1840.

Ravenshaw died at his London residence No 36 Eaton Square, Belgravia, on 14 April 1877, aged 73 years.

Grave 10353 Sq 91. Ledger tomb over brick grave. **Sources:** LCC; MI; Letter from Mrs C. Kelly, archivist, Royal Geographical Society dated 29 April 1982; *General Register H.E.I.C.*

Revd THOMAS FITZARTHUR TORIN RAVENSHAW *MA, FSA, FZS, FRBS* (1829-82) *Anglican Priest, Antiquary and Botanist*

Thomas Fitzarthur Torin Ravenshaw was born in London, the seventh son of John Goldsboro' Ravenshaw, Chairman of the Hon. East India Company, and a younger brother of Edward Cockburn Ravenshaw (q.v.). He was educated at Oriel College, Oxford, and took orders in 1854. He was Rector of Pewsey, Wiltshire from 1857 to 1880.

He was the author of *Flowering Plants of Devon* (1860); *The Festival Psalter [with W. S. Rockstro]* (1863); *A New List of Flowering Plants and Ferns growing Wild in the County of Devon* (1872); and *Antient Epitaphs from AD 1250 to 1800* (1878). He died at 3 Cumberland Terrace, Regent's Park, London, on 26 September 1882.

Grave 10353 Sq 91. Tomb over brick grave. **Sources:** LCC; MI; MEB Vol III 1901; Letter from Mr F. H. Thompson, General Secretary of the Society of Antiquaries 1 Feb 1982; Letter from Mr R. Fish, Librarian, The Zoological Society of London 31 March 1982; *Britten & Boulger's Biographical Index of British and Irish Botanists* nd.

Revd BENJAMIN REEVE (1875-1945)
Baptist Minister and Author

Benjamin Reeve was born in Bermondsey on the 4 March 1875, the son of Benjamin Reeve, warehouseman. He ministered at Maynard Road Baptist Church, Rotherhithe, from 1907 to 1915, and was Assistant Minister at Spurgeon's Metropolitan Tabernacle, Elephant and Castle, in 1916. From 1917 to 1935 he ministered at Vauxhall, and from 1936 to death he was Pastor of Stanmore Baptist Church, Middlesex.

He was the author of *The Divines of Mugtown* - a satirical monograph on church unity (1898); *The History of Maze Pond Sunday School 1801-1901* (1901); *Timothy Richard DD, China Missionary, Statesman and Reformer* (nd); *The Gunpowder Plot and Glorious Revolution* (nd); *Christian Endeavour in the British Isles 1887-1937* (1938).

Reeve was the editor of 'The Christian Endeavour Times' for 21 years (1916-1937) and was President of the British Christian Endeavour Union in 1934-35. He died on 29 May 1945, aged 70 years.

Grave 31598 Sq 166. Headstone. **Sources:** LCC; MI; *Baptist Handbook* 1946 pp 323-4; Information from Howard and Jonathan Reeve 1999.

Sir CHARLES HENRY JOHN RICH *Baronet* (1812-1866)
One of Queen Victoria's Gentlemen-at-Arms

Charles Rich was born at Bossington House, Romsey, Hampshire, on the 22 December 1812, the eldest son and heir of Sir Charles Henry Rich, 2nd baronet. He served as Lieutenant in the 87th Regiment of Foot (Royal Irish Fusiliers) and Cornet in the 14th King's Light Dragoons. He sold his commission on succeeding to the baronetcy in 1857.

Sir Charles, who was one of Queen Victoria's Gentlemen-at-Arms from 1859 to 1861, died at 12 Nottingham Place, Marylebone, on 12 December 1866, aged 53 years. NB. His eldest son, Sir Charles Henry Stuart Rich, 4th baronet, founded the Standing Council of the Baronetage.

Grave 4456 Sqs 136/137. Brick grave (damaged). **Sources:** LCC; MI; MEB Vol VI 1921; *Ridgway's Baronetage of the UK* 1859; Walford, E. *County Families* 1860; Cockayne, G. E. *The Complete Baronetage* 1900/9; Kearsley, H. *His Majesties Bodyguard of the Hon Corps of Gentleman-at-Arms* 1937.

Dame HARRIET THEODOSIA RICH (1833-1870)
Baronet's Widow

Harriet Theodosia Rich was the daughter and co-heir of John Stuart Sullivan of the Madras Civil Service and Devonshire Place, Marylebone. She married Charles Henry John Rich (q.v.) at St Marylebone Church on 27 November 1855. She died at 12 Nottingham Place, Marylebone, on 10 July 1870.
Grave 4456 Sqs 136/137. **Sources:** LCC; MI; Walford, Edward *County Families* 1860; Cockayne, G. E. *The Complete Baronetage* 1900/9.

Revd ROBERT ROBINSON (1814-1887)
Secretary of the London Missionary Society 1865-1884

Robert Robinson was born in London on the 21 January 1814. His Christian education began at Hoxton Academy, and continued at Highbury College, and Chatteris College, Cambridge. He was Pastor of Union Chapel, Luton, from 1843 to 1855, and Pastor of York Road Congregational Chapel, Lambeth, from 1855 to 1865. He was Secretary of the London Missionary Society from 1865 to 1884, and a Director from 1884 to death.

Robinson originated the New Year's Offering Scheme to encourage young men in mission work and to provide for the maintenance of the Society's missionary ships. He was the author of a number of publications including *Link Making in the Home Workshop*. He died at 7 Manor Road, Brockley, 10 January 1887, aged 72 years.
Grave No 12014 Sq 130. Headstone and railings (memorial destroyed by Southwark Council 1980). **Sources:** LCC; MI; MEB Vol III 1901; Waddington, John *Surrey Congregational History* 1866 p 241; *Congregational Year Book* 1888 pp 199-201; Cleal, Edward C. *The Story of Congregationalism in Surrey* 1908.

FREDERICK ROGERS (1846-1915)
Labour Leader & Trade Unionist

Frederick Rogers was born at 11 Gowers Walk, Whitechapel, on the 27 April 1846, the eldest son of Frederick Rogers, a linen draper's assistant. He became an errand boy at the age of ten and was later apprenticed into the vellum bookbinding trade. He joined the Vellum Binders' Trade Society in the 1870s, and became an active trade unionist. He was President of the Vellum Binders' Trade Society from 1892 to 1898, and a frequent delegate to the TUC.

In 1899 Rogers became the first Secretary of the National Committee of Organised Labour for Promoting Old Age Pensions, which first met at Browning Hall, Walworth. In 1900 he was appointed first Chairman of the Labour Representation Committee, forerunner of the present Labour Party.

A pioneer of the University Extension Movement, he took an active part in furthering working class education. He was an Elizabethan orator and scholar, and in association with Sir Henry Irving, appeared in numerous theatres throughout the UK reciting passages from Shakespeare.

Rogers was a familiar figure at Toynbee Hall, and a popular speaker on religion, politics and literature. He believed in the working class and resented the Independent Labour Party's trend towards middle-class leadership. In later life he became completely disillusioned with party politics and found himself opposed to the opinions of most Socialists and Liberals.

He was the author of numerous books and pamphlets including: *James Allanson Picton, A Biographical Sketch* 1883; *The Art of Bookbinding* 1894; *Old Age Pensions - are they desirable and practical?* 1903; *The Early Environment of Robert Browning* 1904; *The Seven Deadly Sins* 1907; and an autobiography, *Labour, Life and Literature* 1913.

He lived many years in East London, but spent the last few years of his life with his sister at New Cross. He died at 29 Bousfield Road on 16 November 1915, and was buried at Nunhead in common grave 32082 Sq 134, on the 23 November. His remains were exhumed and removed to a private grave on the 6 January 1916. The burial rights to the new grave were purchased by his sister Susan Esther Rogers.

Grave No 32203 Sq 137. Cross on a stepped base, bearing the legend 'He lived and died for England.' The grave was vandalised and the cross smashed by persons unknown in August 1998. **Sources:** LCC; MI; DNB; WWW Vol I; Rogers, Frederick *Labour, Life and Literature (autobiography)* 1913; Tracey, Herbert (ed) *The Book of the Labour Party* 1926; Bellamy, Joyce and Saville, John *Dictionary of Labour Biography* Vol I 1972; Kynaston, D. *King Labour - the British Working Class 1850-1914* 1976; Pelling, Henry *A Short History of the Labour Party* 6th edition 1978; Letter from Harold Finch 29 March 1982.

THOMAS ROGERS (c1770-1871)
Centenarian

Thomas Rogers died at No 1 Prospect Place, Union Road, Rotherhithe, in March 1871. His age is shown in the burial records as 101 years. *Grave 3148 Sq 108. Gravestone not located.* **Sources:** LCC.

CHARLES ROLLS (1799-1885)
Still Life Artist and Historical Engraver

Charles Rolls was born at Bermondsey on the 2 June 1799, the fourth son of William Rolls of Marlborough Place, Old Kent Road, floor-cloth manufacturer. He was an excellent draughtsman and helped engrave the plates for the Finden brothers' *Royal Gallery of British Art* 1838-40. He also painted still life subjects exhibited at the British Institution in 1855 and 1857. He died at his residence, Oakdene, Anerley Park, Penge, on 19 November 1885, aged 86 years.
 Grave 8341 Sq 165. Polished granite broken column over brick vault.
Sources: LCC; MI; British census 1881; Benezit, E *Dictionnaire des Peintres, Sculpteurs, Dessinateurs et Graveurs* 1949; *Bryan's Dictionary of Painters and Engravers* 5 vols 1894; Information from Rosemary Burgess.

ROBERT EDWIN RUMSEY (1844-1884)
Professional Cricketer

Robert Edwin Rumsey was born at Greenwich on the 17 February 1844. A lower order right-hand batsman and right-hand fast round-arm bowler, Rumsey played in just three matches for Kent County in 1875. He later took up mechanical engineering. He died at 79 Blackheath Road, Greenwich, on 12 June 1884, aged 40 years.
 Grave 17714 Sq 64. Headstone and footstone *(not located).* **Sources:** LCC; BC 1881; Bailey, Thorn, and Wynne-Thomas *Who's Who of Cricketers* 1984.

Revd JOSHUA RUSSELL (1796-1870)
Baptist Minister and Poet

Joshua Russell was born in Southwark on the 4 March 1796, the eldest son of A. C. Russell, solicitor and clerk to St George's Parish, Southwark. He was educated at St Paul's School and Mill Hill, and became a solicitor in partnership with his father. In 1822 he married Eliza Hoby, the sister of his friend the Revd James Hoby of Maze Pond Baptist Chapel, Southwark. After the death of his father in 1831, Russell abandoned the law profession and became a Baptist preacher at Melksham, Wiltshire. He was ordained in 1835 and became Pastor of Lewisham Road Chapel, Greenwich, in 1841.

In 1850 he visited Baptist Missions in Ceylon and India, and published an account of his travels in 1852. He also published two volumes of poems, the first in 1819, and the second, *The Christian Sabbath, The Way of Life and other poems* in 1853. A second edition was printed in 1860.

Russell ministered at Greenwich for more than 23 years, and died at his

*Headstone over the grave of the Reverend Alfred Saker
African Missionary*

residence on Blackheath Hill on 28 September 1870. Several Baptist ministers attended his funeral including his brother-in-law, the Revd Dr James Hoby and the Revd Dr Edward Bean Underhill, Secretary of the Baptist Missionary Society.

Grave 6250 Sq 99. Tall pedestal monument over brick vault. **Sources:** LCC; MI; *Baptist Union Handbook* 1871 pp 225-227; *Alibone's Dictionary of Authors* 1877.

The Countess RACHEL MOYRA De RUVIGNY (1894-1917) and her mother the Marchioness De RUVIGNY (1870 -1915)

Rachel Moyra De Ruvigny was born in London on the 1 July 1894 the only daughter of the 9th Marquess of Ruvigny and Raineval (see *More Nunhead Notables*). She died at the Clivedon Hotel, Westcliff Parade, Southend-on-Sea, Essex, in September 1917, aged 23 years.

Her mother, the Marchioness De Ruvigny, was born Rose Amalia Cabezos Gaminara, daughter of Poncrasio Gaminara of Genoa and Tumaco, South America. She married the 9th Marquess of Ruvigny and Raineval in 1893 and bore him two sons and a daughter (Rachel). She died at 21 Girdlers Road, Fulham, in March 1915, aged 45 years.

Grave 10412 Sq 42. Small monument (destroyed by Southwark Council in 1980). **Sources:** LCC; Ruvigny, Marquis De *The Titled Nobility of Europe* 1913.

Revd ALFRED SAKER (1814-1880)
Baptist Missionary in Africa

Alfred Saker was born at Borough Green, near Wrotham, Kent, on the 21 July 1814, the son of a millwright and engineer. He attended the village school, and left at the age of ten to work in his father's workshop. In 1830 he became a teacher at the local Baptist sunday school, and was made superintendent.

Following the death of his father in 1838, Saker had to seek work elsewhere and after passing his examination at Woolwich, he was employed at Devonport preparing drawings for the Admiralty. In 1839 he was sent to the Royal Naval Dockyard at Deptford to superintend the erection of machinery there.

In 1840 he married Sarah Ann Helen Jessup *(see biography of Sarah Saker in More Nunhead Notables).*

An ardent Baptist, he wanted to serve Christ in Africa. In 1842 he was accepted by the Committee of the Baptist Missionary Society, and in 1843 he and Sarah sailed to the west coast of Africa. In 1845 they commenced their work among the Dualla towns on the River Cameroons.

Saker was a Baptist Missionary for 37 years, and spent 30 years at Cameroons, where he founded the colony of Victoria in Amboises Bay. He built a church and a school and worked among the Douala people. He also learned to speak and write their language and translated the Bible into Douala.

According to David Livingstone, Alfred Saker was the most important English missionary in West Africa.

Saker returned to England in December 1876, and died at Peckham on the 13 March 1880. He was buried 'amid sunshine and tears' on Friday the 19 March 1880. Among those attending the funeral was his friend and biographer, the Revd Dr Edward Bean Underhill, Secretary of the Baptist Missionary Society. The Revd J. P. Chown conducted the service at the grave side.

Grave 15769 Sqs 131-140. Headstone. **Sources:** LCC; MI; Underhill, Edward Bean *Alfred Saker - a Biography* 1884; Woollacott, Ron *Nunhead's Nonconformists* (unpublished).

HENRY CARL SCHILLER *aka* GREY ANTHONY (1807-1871)
Miscellaneous Writer and Artist

Henry Schiller was born in June 1807 and educated by Dr Styles. He lived in Hull before removing to London, and was music critic for the 'Manchester Musical and Dramatic Review'. A man of many talents, Schiller invented and patented a method for laying deep sea telegraphic cables, and worked with the American photographer John Jabez Mayall, colouring photographs at his Regent Street studio. He was also a miniaturist and portrait painter and exhibited at the Suffolk Street Gallery and Royal Academy in 1844 and 1867.

He was the author of *Christmas at the Grange, a novel in two volumes, by Grey Anthony, illustrated by the author* (1845), and *The Bride of Kynast, a Grand Romantic Opera in 3 Acts, founded on a German story* (1864*).* He also wrote a song about Napoleon Bonaparte and four songs in association with Edward James Loder. His article 'Who painted the Great Murillo de la Merced?' appeared in the August 1870 issue of 'Blackwood's Magazine'. He died at his residence, Manilla House, Peckham Rye, on 4 February 1871.

Grave 11256 Sq 131. Pedestal (with coat of arms). **Sources:** LCC; MI; MEB Vol III 1901; Hamst, Olphar *Handbook of Fictitious Names* 1868; *Alibone's Dictionary of Authors* 1877; Benezit, E. *Dictionnaire des Peintres, Sculpteurs, Dessinateurs et Graveurs* 1949.

Mrs ANNIE LETITIA SCHILLER (d.1887)
Author of a German Cookery Book in English

Annie Letitia Schiller was the wife of Henry Carl Schiller (q.v.). In 1873 she published anonymously *German National Cookery for English Kitchens*. After the death of her husband in 1871 she went to America and lived with her daughter, Madeleine Schiller, alias Mrs Bennett, a concert pianist. She died in New York on 8 March 1887. Her remains were exhumed and interred with those of her husband in June 1891.
    Grave 11256 Sq 131. Pedestal. **Sources:** LCC; MI; MEB Vol III 1901

Sir CHARLES JASPER SELWYN *MA, LL.D, PC* (1813-1869)
Lord Justice of the Court of Appeal

Charles Jasper Selwyn was born at Church Row, Hampstead, on the 13 October 1813, the third and youngest son of William Selwyn QC, legal author. He was educated at Ealing, Eton, and Trinity College, Cambridge, and was called to the Bar at Lincolns Inn in 1840. He was appointed Queen's Counsel in 1856.

    A Conservative in politics, he sat as the Member of Parliament for Cambridge University from 1859 to 1868. In 1867 he was appointed Solicitor-General in Lord Derby's government and was knighted at Osborne in the same year. In 1868 Benjamin Disraeli appointed him Lord Justice of the Court of Appeal in Chancery.

    Sir Charles died at his residence, Pagoda House, Kew Road, Richmond, Surrey, on 11 August 1869. A drinking fountain was erected to his memory at the junction of the Mortlake and Kew Roads.

    NB: His brother, Dr George Augustus Selwyn, was the first Bishop of New Zealand.
    Grave 9864 Sq 91. Tomb over vault. **Sources:** LCC; MI: DNB; MEB Vol III 1901; Walford, Edward *The County Families of the United Kingdom* 1860; Walford, Edward *Greater London* Vol II 1884 p 388; Foster, J. *Men at the Bar* 1885.

JAMES SILVERTHORNE (1812-1852)
Robert Browning's Favourite Cousin

James Silverthorne was born in Camberwell in 1812, the son of William Silverthorne, brewer, and Christiana Wiedemann, sister of Sarah Anna Browning (q.v.). James was the favourite cousin of the poet Robert Browning, and both young men shared a keen interest in art, music and literature. In 1826 James introduced his cousin to the poetry of Shelley.

    The devoted cousins went everywhere together, including to the theatre, and they saw the first London production of Beethoven's *Fidelio* in 1832. James was the only family witness at the secret wedding of Robert Browning to Elizabeth Barrett in St Marylebone Church.

Following the death of his father in 1844, James Silverthorne took over the management of the family brewery in Peckham Road, Camberwell. In 1847 he became seriously ill and the business failed as a result. During the next few years his condition worsened and he died of 'chronic inflammation of the lungs' at the Brewery, North Terrace, Camberwell, on 19 May 1852, aged 40 years.

NB: Robert Browning's poem, *May and Death*, was written 'in affectionate remembrance' of his dear cousin 'Jim'.

Grave 2195 Sqs 95/80. Headstone. Sources: LCC; MI; Irvine, William *The Book, the Ring, and the Poet* - a *Biography of Robert Browning* 1975; Halliday, F. E. *Robert Browning - His Life & Work* 1975; Calcraft, Mairi *Robert Browning's London* - Browning Society Notes Vol 19 1989.

DAVID SMART *MRCS LRCP, LSA, FRAS*, etc. (1848-1913)
Surgeon and Astronomer

David Smart was born at Welwyn, Hertfordshire, on the 18 September 1848, the youngest son of Daniel Smart of Cranbrook, Kent. He was educated at Stamford, Lincolnshire, Denmark Hill Grammar School, Camberwell, and Cranbrook Grammar School, Kent. He became a student of medicine at St Bartholomew's Hospital at the age of 17, and passed his MRCS and LRCP examinations before his 21st birthday. In the early 1870s he acquired the general practice of Dr John Dixon (q.v.) in Grange Road, Bermondsey, and being a keen astronomer, erected a reflector in his garden where he carried out astronomical research.

Smart was a founder Member of the British Astronomical Association and a Member of Council. He was elected FRAS in 1889. He was joint author with Dr Crommelin of *The Perturbations of Halley's Comet in the Past,* and personally observed Halley's Comet at Hove, Sussex, on 22 May 1910. He died at Bermondsey on 27 March 1913, aged 63 years.

Grave 31035 Sq 48. Headstone. Sources: LCC; MI; British Census 1881; *Journal of the British Astronomical Association* Vol 23, Mar 1913; *Memoirs of the BAA* Vol XIX 1914; *Monthly Notices of the Royal Astronomical Society* Vol 74, Feb 1914; *Medical directories*.

Professor ALFRED MONTEM SMITH (1828-1891)
Gentleman of HM Chapels Royal and Composer of Prize-Winning Glees

Alfred Montem Smith was born at Eton on the 13 May 1828, son of Edward Woodley Smith, lay clerk of St George's Chapel, Windsor. He was a chorister at St George's Chapel, Windsor, and at Eton College, and Vicar Choral of Westminster Abbey. He was also Professor of Singing at the Royal Academy of

Music and the Guildhall School of Music.

Smith was a ballad singer with a fine tenor voice and played Damon in Handel's *Acis and Galatea* at the Princess Theatre in 1869. He composed many prize-winning glees including *Sweet Zephyr*.

Professor Smith was a popular lecturer and a Gentleman of HM Chapel Royal at St James's Palace from 1858 to death. He died at his residence, 7 Linden Grove, Nunhead, on 2 May 1891, aged 63 years.

Grave 16943 Sq 17. **Granite ledger tomb** *(removed and destroyed by Southwark Council 1980).* **Sources:** LCC; MI; BC 1881; MEB Vol III 1901.

JOHN ABRAHAM STAIG (1786-1845)
Monumental Mason and Sculptor

In 1838 John Abraham Staig owned a statuary works at Pages Walk, Bermondsey, and was carrying on his trade at Rodney Buildings, New Kent Road, Newington, at the time of his death which occurred on the 23 November 1845.

Signed work by Staig includes a neo-Hellenic monument with angel to Sarah Drew in Streatham Parish Church (1826); a wall tablet to Beriah Drew in Bermondsey Parish Church (1828); and a pedestal monument to Samuel Travers in Nunhead Cemetery.

Grave 531 Sq 141. **Pedestal** *(in ruins) by Frederick Staig of Penge.* **Sources:** LCC; MI; Gunnis, Rupert *Dictionary of British Sculptors 1660-1851* nd; *Trades directories*.

Commander WILLIAM HENRY SYMONS *RN* (1818-1877)
Royal Naval Officer

William Henry Symons was born in 1818, the son of Commander William Henry Symons RN of Plymouth, who fought at the Battle of Trafalgar as Master's Mate on board HMS *Victory*.

W. H. Symons junior entered the Navy in 1832 aged 14 years, and passed his examination at the age of 21. After serving as Mate on board HMS *Blenheim* at the capture of the Bogue Forts in February 1841, and as Acting Lieutenant of HMS *Blonde* in the attack upon Canton, China, in May 1841, he was promoted by the Admiralty to the rank of Lieutenant in October 1841.

In 1842 he was appointed to the *Excellent* gunnery-ship at Portsmouth under Captain Sir Thomas Hastings, and from June 1843, until the spring of 1844, he was employed on HMS *Tyne* in the Mediterranean.

He rose to the rank of Commander and died at 18 Wilson Road, Camberwell, on 7 September 1877, aged 58 years.

Grave 13771 Sq 64. **Headstone. Sources:** LCC; MI; O'Byrne, W. R. *A Naval Biographical Dictionary* 1849.

Miss HARRIET ANN TEBBUTT (1815-1893)
Superintendent of Nurses at the General Hospital, Scutari

Harriet Ann Tebbutt was born on the 21 December 1815. She was one of the forty nurses who, under Mary Stanley's leadership, left London for the Crimea in December 1854. She was appointed Superintendent of Nurses at the General Hospital, Scutari, under Florence Nightingale.

When peace was proclaimed in April 1856, Miss Tebbutt 'who had proved an excellent nurse' returned to England, and at the invitation of Florence Nightingale, stayed at Embley Park. Miss Nightingale wrote, 'as she has only a mother at home, it would give great pleasure if the mother were invited too.'

Miss Tebbutt died at 5 Chichester Street, Upper Westbourne Terrace, London, on 13 December 1893, just one week before her 78th birthday. She is buried in Alfred Mellor's family grave at Nunhead.

Grave 15789 Sq 68. Cross on base. Sources: LCC; MI; MEB Vol III 1901; Woodham-Smith, Cecil *Florence Nightingale 1820-1910* 1952 pp 149, 151, 207.

WALTER THORNBURY (1828-1876)
Journalist, Poet, Novelist, and Historical Writer

Walter Thornbury was born George Walter Thornbury in London on the 13 November 1828, the son of George Thornbury, solicitor. He was educated at Cheam, and on leaving school began writing poetry. At the age of 17 he became a journalist for a Bristol newspaper, and about 1850 he joined the staff of the 'Athenaeum'. He was also a contributor to 'Household Words'.

Thornbury published over twenty biographical and historical works and novels including, *The Monarchs of the Main,* 3 vols (1855); *Life in Spain - past and present,* 2 vols (1859); *British Artists from Hogarth to Turner* 2 vols (1861); *The Life of J. M .W. Turner R.A.* 2 vols (1862); and *A Tour Round England,* 2 vols (1870).

Lovell Augustus Reeve (1814-65), the author and publisher, accused him of plagiarism, claiming that Thornbury's *Life of Turner* was almost entirely a copy of his own work. Thornbury said he wrote the whole of it under the watchful eye of John Ruskin. He is perhaps best known for compiling the first two volumes of the six volume work *Old and New London.* Written in 1872 and 1873, this work, which was his last, was later completed by Edward Walford.

Thornbury died of 'overwork' in Camberwell House Lunatic Asylum, Peckham Road, Camberwell, on 11 June 1876, aged 47 years.

Grave 13937 Sq 59. Headstone with carved medallion portrait *(defaced).*
Sources: LCC; MI; DNB: MEB Vol III, 1901; Hamst, Olphar *Handbook of Fictitious Names* 1868; Kirk, J. F. *Supplement to Alibones's Dictionary of Authors* 1891.

*Monument to Thomas Tilling of Peckham
Jobmaster and Omnibus Pioneer*

Sir JOHN THWAITES *JP* (1815-1870)
First Chairman of the Metropolitan Board of Works

John Thwaites was born on the 24 May 1815 at Meaburn, Westmorland, the son of Christopher Thwaites of Toddy Gill Hall, yeoman. He arrived in London in 1832, and from 1843 to 1855 he traded as a draper in Borough High Street, Southwark. He took an active interest in local and public affairs, and served on the vestries of both Southwark and Greenwich. A devout Baptist, he was Deacon at the Surrey Tabernacle for 16 years.

Thwaites represented Southwark on the Metropolitan Sewers Commission and published *A Sketch of the History and Prospects of the Metropolitan Drainage Question* (1855). In December 1855 he was elected first Chairman of the newly formed Metropolitan Board of Works, forerunner of the London County Council and its successor the GLC, and under his chairmanship the first stage of London's drainage and sewage system was completed by Sir Joseph Bazalgette.

He was knighted at Windsor Castle in 1865, and died at his residence, Meaburn House, Upper Richmond Road, Putney, on 8 August 1870, aged 55 years.

Grave 11039 Sq 162. Ledger over vault. **Sources:** LCC; MI; MEB Vol III 1901; Halliday, Stephen *The Great Stink of London* 1999; Information from Mr Brian Lancaster 1998.

THOMAS TILLING (1825-1893)
Omnibus Pioneer

Thomas Tilling was born at Gutter Edge Farm, Hendon, Middlesex, in 1825, the son of James Tilling, dairy farmer. By 1850 he was a dairyman in Walworth. In 1851, having removed to the nearby village of Peckham, he commenced his famous 'Times' omnibus service to and from the Great Exhibition at Hyde Park. As Peckham grew from a village into a town Tilling's business prospered, and by 1875 he employed no less than 260 workmen and had 700 horses. At the time of his death he owned 7,000 horses and was the largest omnibus operator in South London.

Thomas Tilling, who always described himself as a jobmaster, operated a fleet of hansom cabs as well as omnibuses, ran a riding school in Peckham, and supplied horses to the Fire Brigade, the Police, the Lord Mayor of London, the Metropolitan Board of Works, and the Royal household. He ran his business from his head office Winchester House, a former school building, in High Street, Peckham.

He died at Swanley Cottage, Perry Hill Farm, Catford, on 8 January 1893, aged 67 years. His personal estate was valued at £75,000, an enormous amount in those days.

Grave 6568 Sq 81. Large grey granite pedestal monument. **Sources:** LCC; MI; British Census 1881; MEB Vol III 1901; Blanch, W. H. *Ye Parish of Camberwell* 1875 p 83; Tilling, John *Kings of the Highway* 1957; Barker, T. C. & Robbins, Michael *A History of London Transport* Vol I 1975 pp 39, 89.

Lieutenant JOSEPH TINDALE *RN* (1774-1855)
Royal Naval Officer

Joseph Tindale was born in 1774. He entered the Navy in 1793 as able-bodied seaman on board HMS *Quebec* serving off Ostend and then in the West Indies. In 1795 he was aide-de-camp to Captain Rogers at Grenada, and took part in preventing the French army from entering Georgetown, thereby forcing them to surrender their claims on the colony. As Acting Lieutenant he destroyed two privateers, and once boarded and captured a schooner privateer carrying guns. Mr Tindale was twice captured by the French and held as a prisoner-of-war at St Domingo.

In 1800 he was promoted to the rank of Lieutenant, and in 1804 he was in charge of the *Fly-by-Night,* an armed lugger, engaged in watching the Bolougne flotilla, and conveying dispatches to Lord Keith. For five years, from 1808 to 1813, he was in command of the *Lord Cochrane* hired brig employed in protecting the coasting trade and fishing vessels. During this period he beat off two French privateers and captured another.

Lieutenant Tindale left the sea in May 1814, and was admitted out-pensioner of the Royal Naval Hospital, Greenwich, in October 1837. He died at 5 Blackheath Road, Greenwich, on 2 June 1855 aged 81 years.

Grave 3644 Sq 81. Box tomb. **Sources:** LCC; MI; O'Byrne, W. R. *A Naval Biographical Dictionary* 1849.

JOSEPH TOMLINSON *MICE, MIME* (1823-94)
President of the Institution of Mechanical Engineers 1890-92

Joseph Tomlinson was born in London on the 11 November 1823. His life-long love of locomotives began in 1836 when his father became Passenger Superintendent of the Stockton and Darlington Railway. In 1839 young Joseph was employed by the Manchester and Leeds Railway Company, and by 1846 he was Foreman Engineer with the London and South Western Railway Company at Nine Elms, where he frequently acted as driver of the Royal Train.

In 1852 Tomlinson joined the North Western Railway at Crewe under Francis Trevithick and was appointed Chief Assistant of the Scottish Central Railway. In 1854 he became Assistant Superintendent to the Midland Railway Company, and assisted in adapting locomotives to be fuelled by coal in place of coke.

From 1858 to 1869 he was Locomotive Superintendent of the Taff Vale Company, and afterwards worked as a marine engineer in Cardiff before becoming Resident Engineer and Locomotive Superintendent of the Metropolitan Railway Company in London.

Tomlinson designed the locomotive works at Neasden, which opened in 1883, and constructed railway lines from Moorgate to Aldgate. In 1885 he was a Consulting Engineer in London, and designed and superintended a network of telephone wires all over London for the National Telephone Company.

In 1890, in association with Samuel Swarbrick of the Great Eastern Railway Company, he was employed in the investigation of the management and working of the Taff Vale Railway. Several directors were forced to resign as a result, and Tomlinson was rewarded with a seat on the Board. He was President of the Institution of Mechanical Engineers from 1890 to 1892. He died at 64 Priory Road, West Hampstead, on 22 April 1894, aged 69 years.

Grave 22015 Sq 97. Granite ledger Tomb. **Sources:** LCC; MI; MEB Vol III 1901; *Proceedings of the Institute of Civil Engineers* Vol 117 1894; *Engineering* (obit) pp 621-2 Vol 77 11th May 1894; *Memoirs of the Institute of Mechanical Engineers* pp 163-6 Feb 1894.

ALFRED GLANVILLE VANCE (c1840-1888)
Actor and 'Lion Comique' known as 'THE GREAT VANCE'

Alfred Glanville Vance, whose real name was Alfred Peck Stevens, was born in Surrey about 1840. He was employed first as a solicitors' clerk at Lincoln's Inn, but later opened and ran a dancing academy in Liverpool, after which he went on to become an actor and one of Victorian Music Hall's greatest comic entertainers.

In December 1859 Vance played a clown at St James's Theatre under the name of Glanville in the pantomime 'Punch and Judy'. He made his debut as a comic singer and dancer at the White Lion, Edgware Road, in 1863, and appeared in most of the leading variety theatres. His famous 'heavy swell' character was developed from his original impersonation of the actor Edward

Askew Sothern playing 'Lord Dundreary', a brainless peer, in *Our American Cousin*.

Vance was one of the first artistes to begin his act with a signature tune, which began *Slap bang, here we are again*. In 1866 he gave his address as 'Slap Bang Villa, Peckham', which was in reality 3 Clifton Terrace, where his first wife Jane Catherine Stevens died at the tragically young age of 25 years.

After Jane's death he left Peckham and toured the country for several years with 'Vance's Concert Company'. He played as many as twenty different characters in his shows.

About 1875 Vance married Eunice Irving. His new wife, a Scottish girl from Edinburgh, was only 16 years old. He was her senior by almost 20 years. By 1881 he was living with his young wife at 54 Clapham Road, Lambeth. They had three children, all boys under the age of five.

Songs from Vance's huge repertoire include, *The Converted Cracksman, Fair Girl Dressed in Check, The Beau of Baden-Baden, Act on the Square, Walking to the Zoo, The Chickaleary Cove, Come to your Martha, The Broken Arted Butler, King of Trumps,* and several more Cockney songs. He was a friend and rival of George 'Champagne Charlie' Leybourne.

Whilst impersonating a judge and singing *Are You Guilty?* the 'Great Vance' collapsed and died on the stage of the Sun Music Hall, Knightsbridge, on the evening of Boxing Day 1888. He was buried on Monday, 2 January 1889. Over 1,000 admirers attended his funeral.

Grave 9234 Sq 78. Pedestal monument *(destroyed by Southwark Council for a path widening scheme in 1980)*. **Sources:** LCC; BC 1881; MEB Vol III 1901; DNB; Hartnoll, P. (ed) *Oxford Companion to the Theatre* 1972; Chance-Newton, H. *Idols of the Halls* 1929 reprinted 1975; Busby, R. *British Music Hall - An Illustrated Who's Who* 1976; Hudd, Roy *Music Hall* 1976; Leske, Peter *A Hard Act to Follow - A Music Hall Review* 1978; Billington, Michael *The Guiness Book of Theatre Facts & Feats* 1982 p 152; Honri, Peter *John Wilton's Music Hall - The Handsomest Room in Town* 1985; Law, Jonathan, et al *Brewers Theatre - A Phrase & Fable Dictionary* 1994; Batten, Rex *Nunhead and the Music Hall* 2000 pp 35-39.

JOHN EDWARD VERNHAM (1854-1921)
Church Organist and Composer

John Edward Vernham was born at Lewes, Sussex, in 1921. He was educated under Dr Charles Steggall at the Royal Academy of Music, and first played the organ in St Paul's Church, Walworth, when he was thirteen years of age. He was appointed organist of All Saints Church, Lambeth, at the age of fifteen.

Vernham became Organist and Choirmaster of St Paul's Church, Knightsbridge in 1879, and Professor of Vocal Music at King's College, University of London, in 1889. He published several works on religious music and Christmas carols, including *Novello's Primers Nos 49 and 58*.

He was married to Julia Augarde, pianist. He died at 224 Castellian Mansions, Maida Vale on 2 March 1921, aged 67 years.

Grave 18598 Sq 106. Celtic cross. **Sources:** LCC; MI; WWW Vol II.

Dr CHARLES VERRAL MD (1780-1843)
Physician and Surgeon

Charles Verral was a native of Seaford, Sussex. His surgery was at 15 Howland Street, Fitzrovia, where he specialised in the treatment of spinal disease. He was the founder of the 'Prone System' for the treatment of spinal deformity. He died at 1 Brunswick Place, Wyndham Road, Camberwell, on 20 February 1843, aged 63 years. NB: His son Charles Verral MRCS (1823-80) was Surgeon to the Spinal Hospital in London.

Grave 135 Sq 105. Small pedestal monument with armorial bearings on bronze plaque (in ruins). **Sources:** LCC; MI; *Medical directories*.

JOHN GREEN WALLER *FSA* (1813-1905)
Antiquary, Artist and Brass Engraver

John Green Waller was born in London in 1813, the eldest son of John Waller and Susannah his wife, daughter of William Green MRCS, surgeon of Hoxne, Suffolk. He trained as an artist at the Royal Academy Schools and exhibited genre paintings in London from 1835 to 1848. He also designed a stained glass window to Chaucer in Westminster Abbey, and with his younger brother Lionel Askew Bedingfield Waller (1817-99), he published *A Series of Monumental Brasses from the 13th to 16th Century drawn and engraved by J. G. Waller and L. A .B. Waller* (1840-1846).

Along with Pugin, the Waller brothers led the Victorian revival of the medieval art of brass engraving. They exhibited at the Great Exhibition of 1851 a magnificent brass in the Gothic style which they later used as a memorial to their mother and sister.

In 1861 he was commissioned by the Marquis of Bath to restore a 16th century brass to William Thynne in All Hallows Church.

John Green Waller was a founder of the British Archaeological Association, and the London and Middlesex Archaelogogical Society. He was elected FSA and served on the Council of the Society of Antiquaries of London. He died at 75 Charlton Road, Blackheath, on 19 October 1905, aged 92 years.

Grave 3025 Sq 81. Coped ledger stone. **Sources:** LCC; MI; British Census 1881; Benezet, E. *Dictionnaire des Peintres, Sculpteurs, Dessinateurs et Graveurs* 1949; Meara, David *Victorian Memorial Brasses* 1983 pp 4 & 5, 6-8, 76, 112; letters from Richard Busby and Philip Whittemore 18 and 24 June 1998.

JOSEPH WALLIS (1825-1883)
Prize-winning Musical Instrument Maker

Joseph Wallis was born in Lambeth. He established his musical instrument factory and showroom at 6 Union Street, Borough, before removing to 133-135 Euston Road, St Pancras. At Euston Road he employed twelve men and four boys, and made flutes, pianos, harmoniums, musical boxes, and all kinds of military instruments. His flutes won awards in Paris (1878), Sydney (1879), Melbourne and Adelaide (1881). He died at Ryde, Isle of Wight, on 3 July 1883, aged 58 years.

Grave 7153 Sq 146. Pedestal monument. **Sources:** LCC; MI; BC 1881; Bowers, David *Encyclopaedia of Automatic Musical Instruments* 1972; Bate, Philip *The Flute - a study of its history, development and construction* 1979; *Trades directories.*

THOMAS WALLIS (1821-1894)
Founder of Wallis's Department Store, Holborn

Linen draper Thomas Wallis started his retail business in a small shop in Holborn in 1872. By 1890 he had built a drapery and furniture emporium which dominated Holborn Circus. He resided many years at Sister House, a large mansion at Clapham Common North Side, which was pulled down in 1895. He died at his residence in February 1894, aged 73 years. His department store was destroyed by enemy action in April 1941.

Grave No 17087 Sq 96. **Monument over vault. Sources:** LCC; British Census 1881; Clunn, Harold *The Face of London* 1957 pp 77, 78; Smith, Eric E. *Clapham - an historical tour* 1975 p 5.

JAMES WARD (1800-1884)
Pugilist known as Jem Ward 'The Black Diamond'

James Ward was born at Ratcliffe Highway on Boxing Day 1800, the eldest child of Nicholas Ward, a ballast-getter. He started work aged 12 as a rigger in the East India Docks, and afterwards worked as a coal whipper loading barges. He was a strong young man and took up bare-fist fighting for prize money when he was 16 years old. He was given the sobriquet 'The Black Diamond' because his skin was blackened by coal dust

He fought Tom Cannon at Stansfield Park, near Warwick, on the 19 July 1825. It was a very hot day, and 12,000 spectators watched him knock out his opponent in the tenth round. He was declared 'British Champion'. On the 12 July 1831 he fought and beat Simon Byrne at Willeycott, near Stratford-upon-Avon, and was for the second time proclaimed heavyweight champion.

On retiring from boxing in 1832 he became a tavern keeper in Liverpool, first at the Star Hotel, and afterwards at the York Hotel. He kept the York Hotel for over 20 years, during which time he became a collector of pictures and artist in oils. He exhibited his work at Liverpool between 1846 and 1850. Ward was also a talented musician and played numerous instruments including the flute, piano and violin.

In 1854 Ward returned to London where he kept several public houses during the 1860s. His last pub was the *Sir John Falstaff,* Brydges Street, Strand. In 1860 he executed a large painting of the Sayers v Heenan fight which featured the portraits of no less than 270 personalities of the day, among them champion swimmer Edward Beckwith (q.v.). He retired to the Licenced Victuallers' Asylum, Peckham, and died on 2 April 1884, aged 83 years.

Grave 11980 Sq 51. Headstone. **Sources:** LCC; MI; DNB; MEB Vol III 1901; *Bryan's Dictionary of Painters & Engravers* 5 vols 1904; Benezet, E. *Dictionnaire des Peintres, Sculpteurs, Dessinateurs et Graveurs* 1949; Andre, Sam & Fleischer, Nat *A Pictorial History of Boxing* 1979 pp 31-33.

JOHN WARRINER *Mus.D, FTCL* (1860-1938)
Organist and Music Teacher

John Warriner was born at Bourton Much Wenlock, Shropshire, on the 12 May 1860, the only son of John Warriner of Kirby Moorside. He was educated privately and at Trinity College, Dublin. He worked under the Professors of the Conservatoires of Brussels and Leipseic, and of the Royal Academy of Music.

He was appointed Professor of Pianoforte and Lecturer on the Art of Teaching at Trinity College, London, and was a Member of Faculty of Music and Board of Studies at the University of London.

Dr Warriner was Honorary Secretary and a former President of the London Society of Organists, and the organist at St Matthew's Church, Denmark Hill, Camberwell, for over 50 years (from 1887 to death). He published several books including, *Music for Pianoforte, Organ and Voices; Handbook on the The Art of Teaching applied to Music* 1904; *National Portrait Gallery of British Musicians;* and *Tales of Organist,* etc.

He lived many years at De Crespigny House, Denmark Hill, Camberwell, and died on 12 March 1938, aged 77 years.

***Grave 22447 Sq 137. Celtic cross.* Sources:** LCC; MI; BC 1881; WW 1934; WWW Vol III; *Dictionary of Organs and Organists* 1921; Information from the late Eric Blackwell, organist and former pupil of Dr Warriner, 1982.

Revd JAMES WELLS (1803-1872)
Strict Baptist Minister

James Wells was born of poor parents at Alton, Hampshire, in 1803, and was placed in a workhouse as a little boy even though his parents were still living. He received no education and was illiterate when he left the workhouse. He started work as a farm labourer, and later became a carrier's assistant delivering parcels. He taught himself to read and write.

Wells suffered a serious attack of smallpox when he was twenty-one and nearly died. After a miraculous recovery he became a Christian and joined a Baptist church in Chelsea. He was an enthusiastic preacher, preaching at street corners in Westminster, and in a cats' meat shop.

In 1832 Wells and his growing band of followers moved to Dudley Court, Soho, before renting the Surrey Tabernacle in Borough High Street,

Southwark. In 1840 the old chapel was rebuilt to accommodate the growing congregation. Still more worshippers came, and so in 1865 a brand new tabernacle with over 2,000 seats was built in Wansey Street, Walworth.

Wells was a popular and powerful preacher and his chapel was filled to capacity every Sunday. He was a regular contributor to the *Earthen Vessel* edited by his friend the Revd Charles Waters Banks (q.v.). In 1870 he published a volume of lectures on the *Book of Revelation*.

He died at his residence, 80 Loughborough Park, Brixton, on 10 March 1872, aged 68 years.

Grave 11788 Sq 164. Obelisk over brick vault. *'Erected by his sorrowing congregation'. Mason: D. C. Preston, Nunhead near cemetery.* **Sources:** LCC; MI; *Baptist Union Handbook* 1873 pp 279/81; Whitley, W. T. *The Baptists of London 1612-1928* 1928; Dix, Kenneth *Particular Baptists and Strict Baptists - An Historical Survey* The Strict Baptist Historical Society's Annual Report No 13 1976; Oliver, R. W. *The Life, Teaching and Influence of James Wells* The Strict Baptist Historical Society's Annual Report No 8, 1968.

EDWARD WESTON (1822-1874)
Founder of Weston's Music Hall, Holborn

Edward Weston was born in 1822, the son of Thomas Richard Weston, landlord of the King and Queen Tavern, Paddington Green. He too, became a licensed victualler and was landlord of the 'Six Cans and Punchbowl' public house, High Holborn, from 1853 to 1863.

In 1857 he purchased the National Hall, High Holborn, formerly Gate Street Chapel, which was at the rear of the 'Six Cans' and reopened it as Weston's Music Hall on 13 November 1857.

In 1863 Weston transformed his house and grounds at Highgate Road, Kentish Town, into a 'grand public pleasure garden'. The grounds were spectacularly illuminated by thousands of gas jets. Unfortunately for Weston the customers didn't come in their thousands as anticipated and the whole enterprise flopped. The 'pleasure garden' was later acquired by a railway company for development, and Weston sold his music hall to Sweasey and Holland in 1866. By 1868 he was bankrupt.

Edward Weston was accidentally killed when he slipped and fell in front of a horse and cart. The iron bound wheels of the cart ran over his leg and severed an artery. He was taken to St Bartholomew's Hospital and was pronounced dead on arrival 12 March 1874.

NB: Weston's Music Hall was renamed the Royal by Sweasey, and later became the Holborn Empire. Damaged by enemy action in 1941, the theatre was demolished in 1960 and replaced by an office block.

Grave 2849 Sq 51. Headstone. **Sources:** LCC; MI; MEB Vol III, 1901; Honri, Peter *John Wilton's Music Hall* 1985; Richardson J. *The Kentish Town Panorama* 1986; Batten, Rex *Nunhead and the Music Hall* 2000 pp 11-12.

Mrs MARY FRANCES WILSON (1835-1891)
Dramatic Artist aka Mrs GASTON MURRAY

Mary Frances Wilson was born in Frankfurt, Germany, a daughter of Julio Henry Hughes of the Adelphi Theatre. *(see More Nunhead Notables)*. She married the actor Garstin Parker Wilson, whose stage name was Gaston Murray (q.v.), and performed under the name Mrs Gaston Murray.

She first appeared on the London stage in 1853 at the age of 18, and performed at the Globe, St James's and the Lyceum. A 'capable and intelligent' actress, she played many different parts including Mrs Penguin in 'The Scrap of Paper' and Mrs Primrose in the 'Vicar of Wakefield. She played Mrs Stonehay in Pinero's *Profligate* at the opening of the Garrick Theatre, Haymarket, on the 24 May 1889

Mrs Wilson died at Trent Road, Brixton, on 15 January 1891, aged 56 years, leaving five daughters, two of whom were vocalists. Her husband predeceased her in 1889.

Grave 9718 Sq 27. Ledger. **Sources:** LCC; MI; DNB; BC 1881.

THOMAS WILLIAM WING *JP* (1802-1889)
City Merchant

Thomas William Wing was born in Rotherhithe on the 10 August 1802. He was a Member of Court, Clothworkers' Company, and a magistrate for the County of Suffolk.

He resided many years at 83 Piccadilly, London, and died at 6 Queen's Gardens, Hove, Sussex, on 7 March 1889, aged 86 years.

'He left a name to be blessed by a generation of blind persons for whose benefit he bequeathed in trust - by Will dated 22 October 1884 - to the Clothworkers' Company of London, the sum of £70,000 in Government Annuities for an annual pension of £20 each, without conditions as to sex, age, or place of birth.'

Grave 16304 Sq 70. Huge granite block over brick vault at highest point in the cemetery. Mason: Henry Daniel & Co, Nun-Head. **Sources:** LCC; MI; BC 1881; MEB Vol VI 1921; Kent, William *An Encyclopaedia of London* 1937 p 236.

Captain JOHN ROBERT WOODRIFF *RN* (1791-1868)
Royal Naval Officer

John Robert Woodriff entered the Navy in October 1802 as Midshipman on board HMS *Calcutta*. The ship was commanded by his father Captain Daniel Woodriff, under whom he sailed with a cargo of convicts to Port Philip. He was present at the founding of Hobart Town, Tasmania. In 1805 Woodriff returned to England having circumnavigated the world.

In October 1805, while serving on board HMS *Donegal* at Gibraltar, he assisted at the capture of the *El Rayo* which had been defeated at Trafalgar. He boarded her and remained with her until she was finally wrecked near San Lucar. All on board were either drowned or taken prisoner.

In February 1807 Woodriff was the first man to land at the storming of Montevideo, and took part in the attack upon Buenos Aires under Captain Rowley. As Acting Lieutenant in 1809 he was in command of a slave ship to the Cape of Good Hope. It was a terrible voyage and all on board suffered from lack of food and drinking water.

In 1811 he was promoted to the rank of Lieutenant and commanded a gunboat at the defence of Cadiz and captured two French boats. From 1836 to 1848 he was in charge of a Coast Guard Station with the rank of Commander.

He was promoted to the rank of Captain, and died at 6 Victoria Road, Clapham, on 14 February 1868, aged 77 years.

Grave 4107 Sq 66. Headstone. **Sources:** LCC; MI; O'Byrne, W. R. *A Naval Biographical Dictionary* 1849.

JOHN YEATS *LL.D, FGS, FSS, FRGS* (1814-1902)
Founder of Dr Yeats' Commercial Academy at Peckham

John Yeats resided in Holland for about four years, and lived in the mountains at the base of the higher Alps for about three years. He was elected FRGS in 1854, and FGS in 1869. After leaving Greenwood College, Hampshire, in the mid-1850s, he founded a school in Peckham to train boys for commercial life.

Dr Yeats who was a Member of the Society of Arts for nearly 50 years, filled the office of Examiner in Commercial Geography and History from 1875 to 1888. He received the Society's silver medal for his lecture on *Higher Commercial Education* in 1878.

He was the author of a number of books including, *Natural History of Commerce; Technical History of Commerce; The Growth and Vicissitudes of Commerce in All Ages;* and *Recent and Existing Commerce.* A third edition of each book was published in 1887. Other works by Dr Yeats include, *The Golden Gates of Trade* and *Map Studies of the Mercantile World*, both published in 1890.

He died at 70 Beaufort Square, Chepstow, on 14 June 1902, aged 88 years.

Grave No 4579 Sq 123. Headstone. **Sources:** LCC; MI; Blanch, W. H. *The Parish of Camberwell* 1875 p 265; *Journal of the Society of Arts* June 20 1902; Letter from Mrs Christine Kelly, archivist, Royal Geographical Society 29 April 1982; Letter from Mrs Clarkson, archivist, Geological Society of London, 22 April 1982.

Revd THOMAS YORK *BD* (1819-1894)
Chaplain of St Olave's Union

Thomas York was born at Sudbury, Suffolk, in 1819. He was educated at Queen's College, Cambridge, and took holy orders in 1850. He was Assistant Master at Birmingham and Edgbaston Prep School from 1857 to 1870, and Chaplain of the Queen's Hospital, Birmingham from 1867 to 1879.

In 1879 he was appointed Chaplain of St Olave's Union Infirmary and Bermondsey Workhouse, and from 1884 to death he was Chaplain of St Olave's Workhouse, Horseydown. He died at 78 Union Road, Rotherhithe on 3 October 1894, aged 75 years.

Grave 18212 Sq 75. Headstone. **Sources:** LCC; MI; Crockford; BC 1881; *The Clergy List* 1889.

Commander GEORGE YOUNG *RN* (1785-1857)
Royal Naval Officer

George Young was born on the 14 December 1785, son of Dr Alexander Young MD, a surgeon in the Royal Navy. He entered the Navy in 1800 as Midshipman on board the *Vryheid* prison-ship lying in the Medway, and from 1803 to 1808 he served in HMS *Sceptre* on the East India station. He was promoted Lieutenant in 1808.

As Senior Lieutenant on board HMS *Lion*, he assisted at the reduction of Java in 1810, and took part in Sir Edward Pellew's partial actions with the French Toulon fleet in 1813. From 1841 to 1844 he was employed as an Agent for Transports Afloat. He was Superintendent of the Queen's Ferry Passage, and a magistrate for the Borough of Queen's Ferry, Linlithgow.

Mr Young accepted the rank of Retired Commander in 1846, and died at Copperas Lane, Deptford, 21 April 1857, aged 71 years.

Grave 4103 Sq 52. Headstone. **Sources:** LCC; MI; O'Byrne, W. R. *A Naval Biographical Dictionary* 1849.

Note: The entry relating to Charles Edwin Brown *MICE* (1856-1900), civil engineer, which appeared in the original edition of *Nunhead Notables*, has been omitted from this edition as further research has shown that he died at sea of blackwater fever in 1900, four days homeward from Lagos. Although his name appeared on his family tomb, he was not buried at Nunhead. The monument was removed by Southwark Council c1980.

Grid Plan of Nunhead Cemetery
(Showing square numbers)

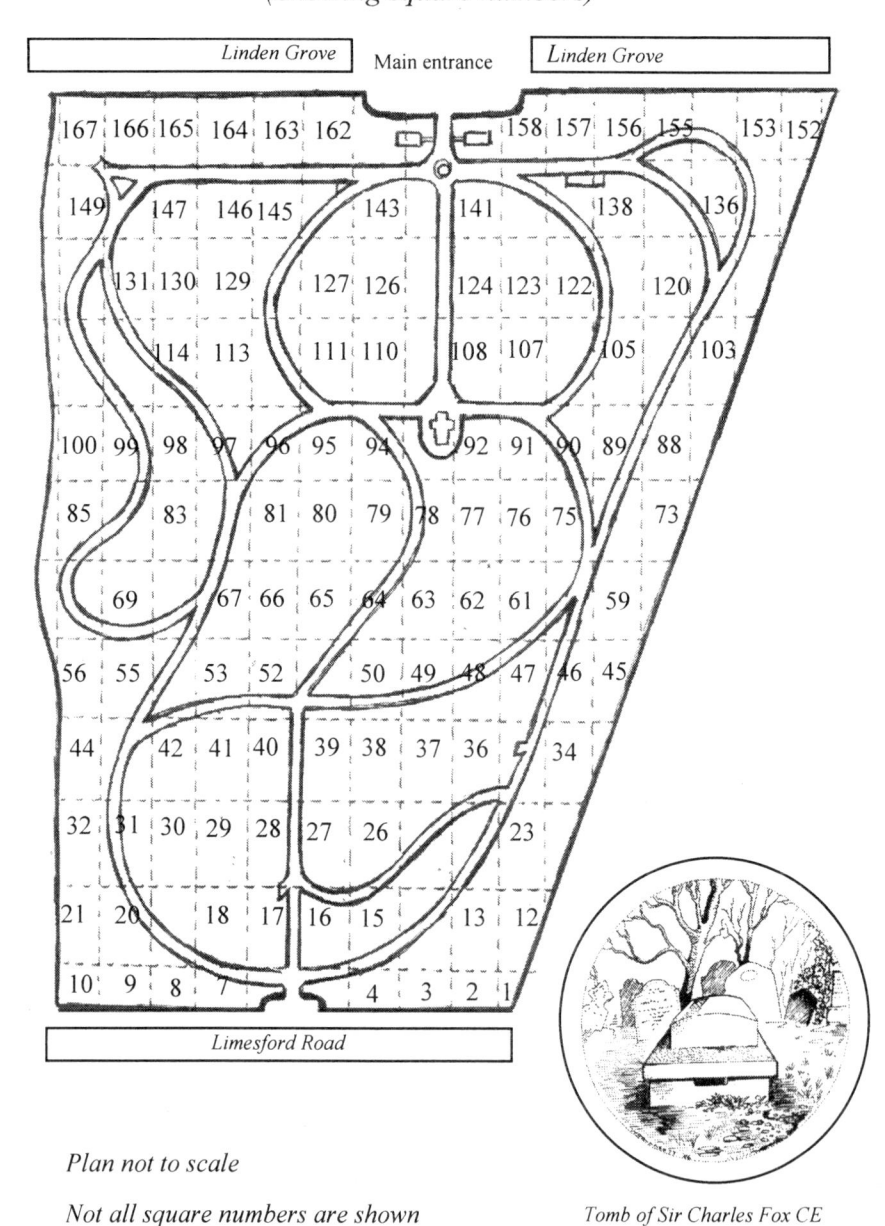

Linden Grove | Main entrance | Linden Grove

167 166 165 164 163 162 | 158 157 156 155 153 152
149 147 146 145 143 141 138 136
131 130 129 127 126 124 123 122 120
114 113 111 110 108 107 105 103
100 99 98 97 96 95 94 92 91 90 89 88
85 83 81 80 79 78 77 76 75 73
69 67 66 65 64 63 62 61 59
56 55 53 52 50 49 48 47 46 45
44 42 41 40 39 38 37 36 34
32 31 30 29 28 27 26 23
21 20 18 17 16 15 13 12
10 9 8 7 4 3 2 1

Limesford Road

Plan not to scale

Not all square numbers are shown

Each complete 'square' is 100 ft by 150 ft

Tomb of Sir Charles Fox CE
(1810-1874)
Square 67

~110~